Collins

Collins Revision

GCSE Foundation Englis'

Revision Gu

420

This book is due for return on or before the last date shown below.

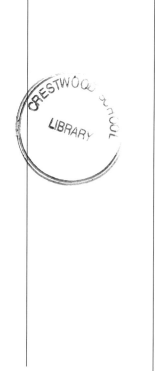

FOR AQA A

Written by Keith Brindle and Kim Richardson

Revision Guide Contents

Exam Practice Workbook Contents

About your AQA/A English exam

Exam papers

- There are two exam papers, Paper 1 and Paper 2.

- Each paper tests some reading skills and some writing skills.

- Each paper is worth 30% of the total marks you can get in your English GCSE.

See the chart opposite: **GCSE English at a glance**.

For more on these exam papers, see:
pages 6–7 (Paper 1, Section A)
pages 28–29 (Paper 2, Section A)
pages 48–49 (Papers 1 and 2, Section B)

The skills you are assessed on

- When the examiners mark your answers, they are looking for certain skills. These are called **assessment objectives**. This book covers all the assessment objectives for Reading and Writing.

- Speaking and listening skills are tested in your coursework, along with reading and writing skills.

The reading skills you are assessed on

In the Reading sections of each paper, you need to show that you:

- **understand what the texts are about**.
  This means explaining their content and purpose. You will need to refer to the texts in your answer.

- **can tell the difference between a fact and an opinion**.
  This means identifying facts and opinions in the text, and explaining how and why they have been used.

- **can write about how information is presented**.
  This means saying how effective you think the texts are at doing their job.

- **can follow an argument**.
  This means explaining what a writer is saying, and how they have put their ideas together.

- **understand the techniques that writers use**.
  This means commenting on the language they use, how they organise their texts and the way they present them on the page.

- **can compare texts**.
  This means explaining how one text is similar to, or different from, another. You need to refer to examples across both texts.

These skills are covered in the first two sections of this book: *Reading Media and Non-Fiction* (pages 6–27) and *Poetry from Different Cultures and Traditions* (pages 28–47).

The writing skills you are assessed on

In the Writing sections of each paper, you need to show that you:

- **can communicate clearly and imaginatively**.
  This means writing so that the reader understands what you are saying and is interested in it.

- **have a clear idea of purpose and audience**.
  This means being able to write in a particular form (e.g. a letter or a newspaper article) and for a particular audience (e.g. young people).

- **can organise your writing**.
  This means using sentences and paragraphs, and giving your writing some sort of structure.
- **can use a range of words and sentence structures**.
  This means using a varied vocabulary, techniques such as repetition and contrast, and different types of sentence for different effects.
- **can punctuate and spell correctly**.
  This means using a range of punctuation, such as full stops, commas and questions marks, and showing that you can spell accurately.

These skills are covered in the final two sections of this book: *Writing Skills* (pages 48–61) and *Types of Writing* (pages 62–87).

GCSE English at a glance

GCSE English Specification A

This tests your reading skills. You will be asked about two or three non-fiction and media texts that you haven't seen before. (pages 6–27)

Paper 1	30% of the total marks
1¾ hours	
Section A Reading non-fiction and media	15%
Section B Writing: argue, persuade, advise	15%

This tests your writing skills. You will be asked to write to argue, persuade or advise. (pages 62–73)

This tests your reading skills. You will be asked about the poems from different cultures in your Anthology. (pages 28–47)

Paper 2	30% of the total marks
1½ hours	
Section A Reading poetry from different cultures and traditions	15%
Section B Writing: inform, explain, describe	15%

This tests your writing skills. You will be asked to write to inform, explain or describe. (pages 74–85)

These are the pieces of coursework that your teacher has asked you to do. They are not covered in this revision guide.

Coursework		40% of the total marks
Speaking and listening		
3 assessed activities		20%
Reading:	Shakespeare	5%
	Prose study	5%
Writing:	Media	5%
	Original writing	5%

Paper 1 Section A: Reading media and non-fiction

Key points

- Paper 1 Section A will focus on **two or three different texts**. You will not have seen these texts before. They will be **media** and **non-fiction** texts.

- In an hour, you will have to answer about **four to six questions**.

- This section of the exam counts for **15% of your total mark**.

Top Tip!

In the Reading questions, no marks are awarded for the accuracy of your spelling, punctuation and grammar. What the examiners are looking for is how well you understand the texts. So focus on your reading skills, and don't worry too much about your writing skills, in this Section.

The texts

- At least one text will be a **media text**. This means a piece of writing from a newspaper, magazine or website, or a printed leaflet, brochure or advice sheet.

- There will probably also be a **non-fiction text** which might not be from the media. This could be an extract from a biography, an autobiography or an information text such as an encyclopedia.

The exam paper

Paper 1 Section A: Foundation Tier

In addition to this paper you will require:
- Text 1: *Need a break? Want a change? Why not try Bognor …?*, from a weekend magazine
- Text 2: *Ancient art of relaxing*, from the *Sunday Express*

> You will be given these texts in full in the exam. They are both media texts. (They are not provided here.)

READING: NON-FICTION AND MEDIA TEXTS

Answer all the questions in Section A.
Spend approximately 60 minutes on Section A.

> Remember to spend up to 10 minutes of this time reading the texts carefully, as well as the questions themselves.

> Note that this question only relates to Text 1. Don't write about both texts here!

1 Re-read Text 1: *Need a break? Want a change? Why not try Bognor ….?*

   a) Why does the writer think it is good to take holidays in Britain? Answer using your own words. *(6 marks)*

   b) Which do you think are the writer's best two points, and why? *(2 marks)*

   c) How does the writer try to make us agree with him? Write about:
- the use of fact and opinion
- any other techniques he uses to make us agree with him. *(6 marks)*

> The marks are given for each question. Use this information to help you time yourself – don't spend a lot of time on this question!

> This question only relates to Text 2.

2 Next, re-read Text 2: *Ancient art of relaxing*.

   a) Who do you think this text has been written for? Explain your opinion. *(4 marks)*

Finally, look at both texts together.

> The final question usually asks you to compare the texts. This means commenting on things that are similar and things that are different.

   b) How do the texts try to interest the reader? Write about:
- each writer's use of language
- presentational devices in *Ancient art of relaxing*. *(9 marks)*

Total: 27 marks

The skills you will be assessed on

The questions that you are asked in Paper 1 Section A will test certain reading skills. This page outlines the skills that are tested (on the left), and explains what you have to do to get good marks (on the right).

The skill you need to show	How to get good marks
1 Understanding what the texts are about *Pages 8–27*	• Find **information** in the texts. • Explain **what the texts are about**. • Recognise their **form**, e.g. a magazine article. • Understand their **purpose**, e.g. to persuade the reader. • Recognise their **target audience** (who they are written for). • **Refer to the texts** in your answer, to provide evidence for your views.
2 Understanding about facts and opinions *Pages 8–9*	• Identify **facts and opinions** in the texts. • Explain **how** they have been used by the writer, and **why**. • Explain their **purpose** in the text and their **effect** on the reader. • Give an opinion on **how successfully** you think the texts do their job.
3 Following an argument *Pages 10–13*	• Understand what a writer says – their **point of view**. • Explain the **key points** they are using. • Identify the **evidence** used to support the key points. • Identify the **techniques** used by the writer to persuade the reader. • Point out what you think makes the argument **convincing** (or not).
4 Understanding the techniques that writers use *Pages 14–21*	• Identify where the writers have used **language to create an effect**, e.g. powerful words, exaggeration, repetition or contrast. • Explain **how** these techniques are **effective**, and **how** they suit the **purpose** or **audience**. • Describe the **structure** of the text and any **presentational devices**, e.g. headlines, pictures, bullet points, and say why they have been used.
5 Choosing the right information and comparing texts *Pages 22–27*	• **Select the right information** from the texts to answer the question, e.g. by skimming or scanning. • Write about the ways in which the texts are **similar** or **different**. • **Refer to examples** across both texts.

Fact and opinion

Key points

- You need to **identify facts and opinions** in one or more texts.
- You need to write about **how they are used**.
- You may need to **compare** the use of fact and opinion in two different texts.

Identifying facts and opinions

- A **fact** is something that can be proved to be true, e.g. *Most people do not smoke*. Usually, there is evidence to back it up.
- An **opinion** is someone's belief, e.g. *Non-smokers have a happier life*. This is someone's point of view – your own view may be different.
- Many texts are a **mixture** of fact and opinion.

The article below is from the magazine *Inside Soap*. The facts are in blue. The opinions are in orange.

'Flamboyant' and 'mouthy' only in the judgement of the writer.

The spokesperson did make this statement.

This is just the spokesperson's own view.

Some people could disagree.

> Emmerdale fans had better brace themselves – **as another member of the** flamboyant **Lambert family is about to descend on the village.**
>
> **Actress Victoria Hawkins – who has previously starred in children's TV show Byker Grove – has been cast as** mouthy **Sharon Lambert, the estranged daughter of Woolpack landlady Val.**
>
> "We're delighted to welcome Victoria to the Emmerdale cast," **said a spokesperson for the soap.** "Sharon's going to cause a lot of trouble for Val. The pair have a very rocky relationship."

It is true that Victoria Hawkins has been in Byker Grove and is going to join the cast of Emmerdale.

Writing about how facts and opinions are used

- Refer to the main **purpose** of the piece. For example, it may be mainly to provide information, in which case facts would be used more than opinions.
- Refer to the **audience** of the piece. For example, it may be people who could buy a product, in which case powerful opinions would be used to persuade them.
- Give **examples** from the text to support your ideas.

The writer's purpose is to give viewers some news about soaps, but also to persuade them to watch the programme. So there is a mixture of fact and opinion. The facts about how Sharon Lambert is related to the landlady Val are surrounded by opinions about the characters ('flamboyant', 'mouthy'), what is going to happen ('going to cause a lot of trouble') and the effect on the fans (they 'had better brace themselves') ...

Good Points

- The student explains why fact and opinion are both used, by referring to the writer's purpose.
- Suitable examples are used (or referred to) to support the ideas.
- This is likely to develop into a Grade C answer.

The next extract is from the *Yorkshire Evening Post*.

- In this extract, there are more facts than opinions.
- The purpose of the article is to report a story, not to sell something.
- The writer includes opinions from Graham.
- Graham uses facts to make the opinions believable, and to encourage people to support them.

Top Tip!

Remember that facts can be used in different ways. Some facts simply present information. Others back up a writer's opinions, so their purpose is more persuasive.

A couple celebrating their 40th birthdays have asked for donations to charity instead of presents.

Graham and Chris Lingard of Ilkley both support Christian Aid, the churches' charity which raises money to help struggling Third World countries.

Their birthdays are close to each other and they decided on a joint party as part of this week's nationwide Christian Aid collection week.

Graham said: 'We both wanted to highlight how unfair our world is, and support a charity that works to help change this injustice.

'The problems facing Africa are hard for us even to imagine. Currently – due to chronic poverty, coupled with recurring drought – 38 million people simply do not have enough to eat. In 2005 AIDS alone killed over 2 million people in sub-Saharan Africa,' he said.

opinion — 'The problems facing Africa are hard for us even to imagine.

fact — In 2005 AIDS alone killed over 2 million people

Comparing texts

If the use of facts and opinions has to be compared in two texts, follow this plan:

- Paragraph 1: Write about the **first text** and how facts and opinions are used.
- Paragraph 2: Write about the **second text** and how facts and opinions are used.
- Paragraph 3: **Compare the two texts** and discuss whether their use of fact/opinion is the same or different.

This student is comparing how fact and opinion are used in the articles from *Inside Soap* and the *Yorkshire Evening Post*. This is how she starts the three paragraphs:

(Paragraph 1) The first text relies heavily on opinions, for example ... This is because the purpose of the text ...

(Paragraph 2) The second text, by contrast, begins with facts ... This is because ...

(Paragraph 3) In conclusion, the texts are very different, but each suits its purpose ...

Task

Use the sentence starters above to complete this task:
Compare how fact and opinion are used in the articles from *Inside Soap* and the *Yorkshire Evening Post*.

READING MEDIA AND NON-FICTION

Following an argument

Key points

- An **argument** is a structured way of putting forward an opinion about something.

- You need to show that you can **follow an argument**.

- This means identifying the writer's **point of view**.

- It will also mean showing **how the argument has been put together**. This means commenting on its **structure**, **language** and any **techniques** used.

Top Tip!

Don't simply repeat the content of the argument. You will need to put the argument into your own words, and comment on how it is structured and how language is used.

The writer's point of view

- The writer's **point of view** is their **attitude** to the subject of the text. For example, the point of view of the writer of the article below is that people are obsessed by watching sport.

- Identifying the point of view will help you explain the text's **purpose**, or why it was written. The writer's purpose in the article below is to show how bad the situation is, and to say what to do about it.

Structure

- When commenting on the structure of an argument, try to identify:

  – the **introduction**. This sets out the subject of the argument and shows the writer's viewpoint.

  – the **key points**. The argument is developed with some key points, usually backed by **evidence**. Often there is one key point in each paragraph.

  – the **conclusion**. This sums up the writer's point of view. It is a final statement to persuade the reader.

- Also try to spot where the writer attacks the **opposite viewpoint**. They do this to make their own argument stronger.

Look at the article about sport below and on page 11. (Only the first and last paragraphs have been given in full.) The notes show how the writer has structured the argument.

Paragraph 1: the writer's main point – that we are obsessed by sport.

What is it that makes people believe that watching sport is the most important activity known to man? Let's face it, we only live for seventy years – eighty if we're lucky – and yet so many people waste so much time watching pretty brainless bodies chasing a ball round a patch of grass; and often spend hundreds of pounds for the privilege. Failing that, they are glued to the game on TV. And when they are dead, what then? A life has been wasted, potential squandered, and nothing has been achieved.

Football fans, of course, see it differently …

This line of argument, however, is nothing short of ludicrous …

How many goals do we remember? How many service aces justify the time we spend watching …?

There must, surely, be more we could be doing …

Paragraph 2: the opposing viewpoint – that it's great to watch sport.

Paragraph 3: the opposing viewpoint is attacked.

Paragraphs 4 and 5: these add some key points to develop the argument.

Paragraph 6: the conclusion – that we need to change this situation to make society better.

So, what is the solution? In Britain we need to change the consciousness of the nation. Firstly, people need educating to realise that we could do more useful things to develop ourselves and – just imagine! – help others. Secondly, we need to remove the cult of the sport star and, instead, lay much more emphasis on those who do something worthwhile. How much better it would be, for example, if children grew up wanting to be a doctor, rather than Wayne Rooney.

Writing about structure

How could you summarise the way the argument in the article about sport has been put together? You could begin like this:

The article begins by pointing out that we waste our time watching sport. The writer makes his point of view very clear at the start, by making sportsmen seem unintelligent (we watch 'pretty brainless bodies chasing a ball'). We could do more with our lives: 'nothing has been achieved'.

The writer does go on to say that the fans have a different view. But immediately he attacks this view by suggesting it is 'ludicrous' or crazy. This helps to build up his own argument.

The middle section of the article adds further points to support the writer's argument. These are . . .

The article ends with a powerful conclusion. The writer suggests ways we could change things and improve the quality of our lives. The final sentence makes a strong contrast between being a doctor and being a footballer.

Grade C

Good Points

- This answer shows clear understanding of the structure: the beginning, the development of the argument, and the conclusion.
- It is organised logically – commenting on each section in turn.
- It quotes evidence from the text to back up the points made.

READING MEDIA AND NON-FICTION

Language

- Note how the language in an argument suits the **audience**:

  – *Hey, guys, don't diss me* is aimed at a young, cool audience.

  – *Those on the margins of society should not be condemned* is aimed at an intelligent, old-fashioned audience.

- Note how the language suits the **purpose** of the text:

  – If the argument is a proposal by a supermarket to build a large out-of-town store, the language will be calm, formal and logical.

  – If the writer is aiming to amuse the audience as much as persuade them, the language might be more exaggerated.

> **Top Tip!**
>
> When commenting on language in an argument, always refer to the purpose and audience of the writer.

Pages 14–17 (more on language use)

Techniques

- Identify the **techniques** that writers use to convince the reader.

- Some of these techniques for building an argument are described below.

  – **rhetorical questions**: questions asked for effect, that do not expect a reply, e.g.

  Don't we know this is lunacy? Is there nothing we can do?

  – **exaggeration**: overstating the case, to make the point even more strongly, e.g.

  There must be millions of rats just praying this law is passed and the sewers remain uncleaned ...

  – **examples, repetition and lists**: details selected or emphasised to support a point, e.g.

  example:

  For example, half my children's presents lie unused after Christmas.

  repetition:

  Young people agree. Middle-aged people agree. Even older people agree.

  list:

  There are so many problems: homelessness, drug-taking, violence ...

  – **personal stories or anecdotes**: brief stories used to show what happens, or what happened, e.g.

  Only last week, I was approached by a homeless person on my own street. She was not begging, however. She explained to me that ...

  – **quotations**, usually from people with particular knowledge of the subject, e.g.

  "In my role as mayor, I see what happens and know what is wrong ..."

  – **contrast**: setting contrasting points or images beside each other for effect, e.g.

  On one side there are the rich, arguing for lower taxes. On the other side sit the poor, who know that more money has to be raised to protect the health service.

  – **humour**, such as sarcasm: used to get the reader on the writer's side, e.g.

  This is the greatest victory since Waterton Road Under 7s trounced Snapethorpe in the Lupset Women's Group's Minor Footie League in 1959.

> **Top Tip!**
>
> When you identify the techniques a writer has used to build an argument, use a quotation to make the technique clear for the examiner. Even better, explain how the technique helps the writer make their point.

You can see some of these techniques being used in this magazine article. A middle-aged man writes about what it is like to grow older.

They say that age is a state of mind. I think age happens when you can no longer watch pop music on TV without cringing. I was brought up on *Top of the Pops* – in fact I lived for my Thursday evening fix of the latest sounds. I was devastated when the show was axed. What do kids watch now? I decided to find out by sitting with my own children one evening.

Shock and dismay. The channel was called 'Kiss' – that should have been a warning in itself. And instead of some friendly, reliable old DJ fronting the show, there was a continuous stream of what appeared to be semi-naked girls faintly disguised as pop artists.

'How old is she?' I asked my son, aghast, as I watched one of them, who looked as if she should be in school.

'Chill, dad.'

'She just giggles and screams. And she's wearing underwear.'

'So? Don't we all?'

Then, the performances.

'Why do they do that?'

'What?'

'The rappers … Their hands … Why do they do that with their hands? No drier in the toilets?'

'It's what they do.'

'But why?'

It's weird when a whole part of your life has passed you by, but, frankly, you don't care because you are happier with your memories of Tony Blackburn and the Beatles and the Eurovision Song Contest and singers who had hair and sang and didn't have bodies with rings all over, like chain mail.

Of course, it's next stop afternoon bingo. Then a stair lift. And, frighteningly, what comes after that …?

Maybe I'll breathe deeply and try to appreciate the girls and the rappers. While I still can.

Annotations (left):
- **contrast** of the 'old DJ' and the 'semi-naked girls'
- **personal story** to help explain his point of view
- **humour** to win the reader over

Annotations (right):
- **listing** lots of **examples** can be powerful
- **exaggerated** picture – overstating the case for effect
- **rhetorical question** – he knows the answer (death)
- **humour** – note also the short phrase to end

Question

What does the writer of this magazine article have to say about growing older, and how does he build his argument?

Briefly explain:

- the writer's point of view
- the structure of the argument
- how he uses language and techniques to win the reader over to his point of view.

Language

Key points

- You will be asked to write about the **language** used in one or two of the texts.

- This means picking out the most **obvious features**, such as:
  - sentences and paragraphs
  - vocabulary (the words used)
  - punctuation
  - imagery
  - the style of the language.

> **Top Tip!**
>
> When commenting on the language of a text, don't try to write about the whole text. Focus on two or three key points, and go into detail on each one.

Sentences and paragraphs

- Notice the **length of sentences**, and the way they are **constructed**. This can produce different effects, such as:

  - **Short sentences** sometimes suggest speed or excitement, e.g.

  He ran forward. The ball fell at his feet. He shot.

  - **Long sentences** can help describe an event, building to a climax, e.g.

  The crowds gasped as the top of the mountain blew away, clouds of ash shot hundreds of feet into the sky and rivers of lava, terrifying in the early dawn, shot upwards, then cascaded down into the valley.

- **Paragraphs**, too, can create different effects:

  - **Very short paragraphs** can be used to pick out the main details, or to speed the reader on. Popular newspaper articles often have short paragraphs so that they can be read more easily.

  - **Longer paragraphs** can provide more detail and analysis. Articles in more serious newspapers often have longer paragraphs.

> **Top Tip!**
>
> Look out for paragraphs of very different lengths. A one-sentence paragraph after a long paragraph, for example, aims to grab the reader's attention.

Vocabulary

- The sort of words used in a text can tell you a lot about the **purpose** of the text:

  - Powerful **adjectives**, such as 'fantastic' and 'appalling', are often used to **persuade** the reader.

  - **Commands**, such as 'follow' and 'begin', suggest that the writing is giving **instructions** or **advice**.

  - Words like 'since' and 'because' suggest that the writing is **explaining** something.

  - Words like 'however', 'nevertheless' and 'indeed' may come from writing that is **arguing** a case.

- The words used can also tell you about the **audience** for a text:

  - **Longer words** suggest a text is aimed at an intelligent readership.

  - A text containing **modern vocabulary**, for instance dealing with ICT and communications, could be targeting younger people or those in the industry.

  - A text containing **slang** might be aimed at teenagers.

  - Vocabulary associated with a **specific subject** would be used in a text aimed at specialists. For example, a geography textbook will contain lots of geographical terms.

> **Top Tip!**
>
> Notice any word that seems powerful or unusual. There will be a reason why the writer has used it, and it will be worth commenting on. For example, *The dog howled incessantly* is more powerful than *The dog barked and barked*. The effect is to emphasise the unhappy sound the dog made.

Punctuation

• Look out for exclamation marks and question marks. They have a purpose, e.g.

HOLLY HITS OUT!!

> The double exclamation mark attracts attention and suggests excitement.

WHY AREN'T WE BEING TOLD THE TRUTH?

> The question also attracts attention by addressing the reader directly.

Imagery

• **Imagery** means using words to paint a picture. If a writer describes her son's room as a 'dustbin', she is using the image of a dustbin to make you realise how messy the room is.

• **Similes** and **metaphors** are examples of imagery.

This short extract has three examples of imagery:

> similes – the 'like' shows something is being compared to something else (an image)

> They held us in a small room. We felt like condemned men and smelt like battery hens. We had no idea of the day or the time and dreaded the dull echoes of sharp boots and the crank of the lock on the door. It was an eternity of torture ...

> metaphor – being imprisoned is described as a 'torture'

Top Tip!

When you comment on language, use the correct technical term if you can (e.g. simile), but the main thing is to describe what effect it has, and why the writer has used it.

Look at how this student has commented on the use of language in the extract above:

> The writer uses imagery to show what their life was like. The simile 'like condemned men' stresses their desperate situation. Another simile ('smelt like battery hens') shows the terrible conditions they were kept in. They were like animals.
> Finally, the metaphor 'eternity of torture' is used to express how long and painful it must have seemed to them at the time.

Grade C

Good Points

• Precise examples are given, backed up by quotations from the text.
• The effects of the language are discussed, not just identified (e.g. 'the simile ... stresses their desperate situation').
• Some technical terms are used, e.g. simile, metaphor.

READING MEDIA AND NON-FICTION

Style

- A text may be **formal** – with a more serious tone, e.g. serious newspaper articles, job applications. Here are some common features of a formal text:
  - close attention to all the rules of English
  - more difficult words
  - longer sentences.
- A text may be **informal** – with a warmer or chattier tone, e.g. emails, advertisements and light magazine articles. Common features include:
  - less attention to the rules of grammar and punctuation
  - the use of slang
  - simpler and more direct words and sentences.

> **Top Tip!**
>
> Always give examples to back up your comments, e.g.
>
> The first text is formal, using sentences like 'The government has taken a stance which ...', while the second text is less formal and targets drug users: 'Get real ...'

Stylistic techniques

- Writers use different stylistic techniques to create effects:
  - **addressing the reader** directly (especially with **rhetorical questions**), to add impact:

  Can this be acceptable?

  - **emotive language**, which touches the reader's feelings:

  They are tiny and cold and they are starving.

  - **exaggeration**:

  The royal family eats nothing but caviar for breakfast.

  - **contrasts**:

  The seabirds sing, while the fishermen starve.

  - **colloquial language**, as if people are chatting:

  If you want to pull, you have to impress the lads.

  - **suggestion**, where things are suggested rather than clearly stated:

  He met the girl of his dreams. He didn't come home that night.

  - **examples** and **quotations**, to give credibility to what is written:

  Only yesterday, a shop assistant said to me ...

  - **humour**, to get the audience on the side of the writer:

  There was more life in my popcorn than in this film.

  - **lists**, for emphasis:

  She packed the potatoes on top of the bananas, the bananas on top of the tomatoes and the tomatoes on top of the eggs.

> **Top Tip!**
>
> Identifying features like these and commenting on their effect gets you extra marks in the exam. Practise finding them in the magazines you read. Work out what effect the writer is trying to create.

This extract from a newspaper article uses several of the techniques above.

> So, the Prime Minister claims that he has an excellent track record, does he? An excellent track record of what – destroying all areas of British life?
>
> People are paying taxes they can't afford, waiting in traffic that never moves, facing ever-mounting debt and an impoverished old age ...

You could comment on the style like this:

The writer begins by addressing us directly, which gets our attention. When she says 'claims', it makes us think it's not true. The next sentence is another rhetorical question, which contrasts the 'excellent' track record with the actual destruction of British life. Exaggeration is used here ('all areas') for added effect.
The list of three examples helps to build up the evidence against the Prime Minister. Exaggeration is used again ('never moves') and some emotive language when the writer refers to poor old people. This aims to get us on her side.

Grade C

Good Points

- The effect of the language is described.
- The purpose of the writer is referred to.
- Quotations are used to prove the points being made.
- Some technical terms are used, e.g. rhetorical, emotive.

Question

This extract comes from *Take a Break* magazine. Its aim is to attract people to visit Capri.
Some of the features of the writer's language have been highlighted in red.
Match them up with the list of features in the box.

Gaze and laze

Take a break where the sun always shines

All eyes turn to the sea on this 30-mile stretch of Italy's western shore, considered one of the most beautiful coastlines in the world, where Campania gazes out into the Tyrrhenian reaches of the Mediterranean.

It takes in Sorrento, Positano, Salerno and Amalfi – which gives it the local name *Costiera Amalfitana* – and even extends into the sea.

Sitting off the coast like a satellite at the end of the peninsula, the island of Capri is just a 20-minute cruise away from Sorrento. Fram the port of Marina Grande it's a short ride by funicular railway to the labyrinth of narrow alleyways that make up Capri town.

But it is at Anacapri, the island's second town, that you'll find Capri's very own Garden of Eden, where mythological statues sit like sentinels surveying the deep blue waters. Or where classically draped figures from Italy's past appear to hold command over clouds fleeing across the contrasting blue of the sky.

Find an example of:

- exaggeration
- a simile
- direct address to reader
- a list
- a metaphor
- another simile

Layout and presentational devices

Key points

- You need to understand how **layout** and **presentational devices** are used in media texts.

- Layout means the way the page is arranged. Presentational devices are the different features that are used to create the layout, such as pictures and headlines.

- You will be expected to write about **why** these particular devices have been used.

Identifying the features

- Some common features used in media texts include:

strapline – a second-level headline which gives more details

introductory paragraph could be in bold print or with the first word capitalised

subheading – minor heading used to give a summary, or break up the text, or grab the reader's attention

heading – note the size and style. The main heading is called a headline. Here, block capitals are used for emphasis.

photograph – illustrations are often an important part of the design. How do they relate to the text?

caption – the text under a photograph or diagram which helps us understand it

columns – text often in columns to make it easier to read

PEACE AT LAST?

PM set to sign treaty at end of historic talks

ONLY LAST YEAR, the prospect of a resolution to the conflict seemed remote. Now, with all parties in agreement, there is a chance of peace.

Last chance

The Prime Minister faced tough questions yesterday

logo – an image that represents a product or company

font – the style of the typeface. The style, size and colour can vary throughout a text.

bold, italics, underlining – different ways of making words stand out

quotation – taken from a reviewer of the club and set apart, to make it stand out

slogan – a word or phrase linked with a product, so you can remember it

photographs and graphics – different kinds of illustration used for different purposes, e.g. the map to help people find the club

NITE STAR

The brightest club in town

8:30pm till 1:00am
Monday – Saturday

Tickets £10

High Street
New Street
NITE S.TAR
Main Road

How to find us

"Nite Star? It's heaven!"

Writing about presentational devices

- Don't just describe what is on the page. Talk about **why** the text has been designed in a particular way. What **effect** does each device have?

headline – grabs attention of reader

photos – show smiling people because they are happy in their work

bold introduction – to mark out the description of each person, before their actual words are given

Q: Are we a nation of workaholics?

I work hard because I have no choice

IVANA STRUKIEL, 38, is single, a cleaner and lives in North London. Born in Poland, she moved to England two years ago. My stresses are not the stresses of a managing director in the City, but they are financial and physical: stooping down, straining my back, carrying heavy equipment every day. You have to make a lot of sacrifices just to survive in a city like London. The cost of living is very high and it's hard to find work. I would like to be an administrator or a translator but, because I have bills to pay, I am a cleaner. I work probably 45 hours a week and clean eight houses to be able to afford my lifestyle – which is a room in a shared household with many other people. I'm not complaining. It's OK, it is

Workaholics can't make their minds up

MARKSTEEN ADAMSON, 40, is a founding partner of advertising agency ArthurSteenHorneAdamson (www.ashawebsite.com). He is married, has four children and lives in Cheltenham. I worked for years in advertising

Long hours don't produce better work

RACHEL OSAIGBOVO, 31, is co-director of the Festival of Youth Arts (www.festivalofyoutharts. org.uk). She lives in London with her partner. You shouldn't need longer than nine-to-five to

pull-quote – stands out because (a) larger, (b) in orange. It highlights the actual words of each person interviewed.

block capitals – emphasise the people's names

overall design – text in columns, orange and black used

Here is how one student commented on the way layout and presentational devices are used in the article:

> The article is designed in three columns because it gives three interviews. Two of them have photos, which show people who are not workaholics and so are happy with their jobs. Each column begins in the same way. First there is a quotation, to show the most important thing that the person thinks about the question. Then there is a paragraph in bold, which introduces the person and gives their name in capitals to make it stand out. Then their speech is given in ordinary 'look', as this is the main part of the article. The orange touches, which make the article feel "cheery", alongside the smiles in the pictures, make this an attractive piece of writing.

Grade C

Good Points

- The different presentational features are identified, even if the correct terms are not always used.
- The purpose of all the features is given.
- It includes an opinion about how effective the design is.

Question

Choose an article from your favourite magazine. List all the presentational devices used, and explain why they are used. How effective are they?

How to refer to the text successfully

Key points

- To support your answers, you need to **refer directly to the text**.
- The references should be **relevant** to the point you are making.
- Make **brief quotations** from the text, and **explain** what they show.

Quoting and referring

- Sometimes you may want to **quote** some words **directly** from the text. Put inverted commas around any words you quote. Include the quotation as part of your sentence:

  The writer emphasises how delicious the ice cream is. 'Mmmm'. ✘

  By placing 'Mmmm' in a paragraph of its own, the writer emphasises how delicious the ice cream is. ✔

- Sometimes you might want to identify a number of words to prove your point:

  The writer emphasises how delicious the cream is when she says: 'Mmmm. That was fantastic!'

- Each quotation should be relevant – you are quoting to **back up your own points**. Don't quote because you can't think of anything else to say!

- Try to add a **comment** about each quotation to **explain** why you have included it.

- Sometimes you may want simply to **refer to a detail** in the text, but not quote it directly. You can use your own words:

  The writer points out that no other ice cream has the same quality and price.

Top Tip!

Make sure you **read the question carefully** to see exactly what you have to do. You may be asked to read only part of a text. Notice helpful information, such as:

*Read the **opening paragraph** and **explain** …*

*Find **three facts** and say **how they support** what the writer believes …*

*What **techniques** are used **to convince** the reader that …*

Top Tip!

Try not to quote large amounts of text – it won't gain you marks.

Look at this extract from *Africa Today*, and how the student analyses it.

> When she spoke to the conference, Celia Bowers was quite clear about what her department was going to do. She felt that in just two years' time people would notice the difference: the quality of water would be improved and, indeed, the places in which people lived would be transformed …

> The writer makes Celia Bowers seem confident from the start. He says she 'was clear' about her objectives. This suggests she has thought through her ideas, and can put them across very well. He describes some of the improvements that are planned. He moves from the quality of the water to the complete transformation of the region. This shows how wide-ranging and effective her plans are.

Grade C

Good Points ✔

- Either direct quotations or references to the text are used to support each point.
- Comments explain why the references have been made.

Task

Improve the student's answer on page 19 by adding a quotation from the text. Make sure it is relevant, and that you add a comment which backs up your quotation.

Analysing text types

Key points

- There are **different kinds** of media and non-fiction texts, such as newspaper stories, websites and travel writing. These are called **text types**.

Page 6

- Each text type uses particular kinds of **language**, **layout** and **presentational features** to achieve its purpose.

- To get good marks, you need to show that you understand **how** and **why** these devices are used.

News reports

- The main purpose of news reports is to **give information**. Many also aim to **entertain**, especially stories.

Page 18

- Many **presentational devices** are used to attract the reader.

- **Key points** of the story are given first. Later paragraphs give more **detail** and include **quotations** from the people involved.

Look at this report from *The Sun*.

Strapline tells you more about the story.

Catchy **headline** put in capitals.

Picture shows ship looking old/ready to scrap – lots of grey.

'Protest' shows the human interest, and suggests conflict.

Short paragraphs (one sentence each) make text easy to read.

'Toxic rust-bucket' – strong language makes ship sound dangerous.

'TOXIC' RUST-BUCKET IS HERE

Protest as ship docks

A RUSTING ghost ship dubbed a "toxic time bomb" arrives in Britain yesterday — to be greeted by crowds of angry environmental protesters.

The Caloosahatchee, one of four redundant US Navy vessels being sent here to be scrapped, docked at Hartlepool, Teesside.

Protesters say they are packed with toxic chemicals and must be returned to America.

The Government allowed the ships to dock in Hartlepool — but says the local firm that won the contract to scrap them must not start until a legal row over their fate is decided.

Protester Barbara Crosbie, 36, from Hartlepool said yesterday: "Ninety per cent of people living here don't think this is right. We're angry and want all these ships sent back."

First paragraph sums up the story.

Later paragraphs give more background and detail.

Final paragraph is a **quotation** from an eye-witness, for human interest.

Text box makes report stand out.

People give scale and show it's a human story as well.

Web pages

- Web pages have a variety of purposes, but often **sell** products or give **information**.
- **Design** is an important feature – web pages have to **attract** the reader.
- **Text**: writing has to be **brief** and **punchy**, as readers have a short attention span as they surf the net.

main heading to show what this page is about: the holiday section of 'lifestyle'

main image to attract attention: suggests fabulous foreign holiday

commands to get reader to click on text: 'get inspiration', etc.

name of website provider

search button

main navigation bar with links to other content

questions to grab reader's attention: 'What's your holiday money worth?' etc.

active links in green (matching colour of main photo)

short snatches of text to tempt the reader in for more

logo stands out

pictures show variety of content and are attractive

wordplay (lots of 'v's) to amuse/ attract reader

Here is one student's analysis of this web page:

This web page is designed to interest people thinking about a holiday. So it gives lots of information about different places, and pictures to attract the reader. The main picture makes you go 'Wow' and will attract any traveller, there are also some smaller pictures which show other places to go to and things to do.

The text is written to attract the reader as well. Phrases like 'Try ...', 'Tell us ...' aim to get the reader to do things. There are quite a lot of questions as well, such as 'What's your holiday money worth?' These speak directly to the reader and make them want to answer the question by reading further. Finally there is also some 'fun' writing, like 'Va va voom cities' which is another way of keeping the reader's interest.

The website is organised so that people can find their way about the site easily. There is a navigation bar on the left, and lots of links everywhere to other pages. The link text is in green to make it stand out. Above all, there aren't any long bits of writing, as readers don't have time for this. Instead lots of headings are given (like 'World's best beaches') and the first bits of text, just to give readers the flavour of the full articles. It's teasing them really, but very effective.

Grade C

Good Points

- The answer covers the language, images and the overall presentation.
- It takes into account the purpose and the audience of the website.
- It refers to relevant details from the text to back up the points made.

Top Tip!

Whenever you analyse or discuss a media text, you are likely to have to cover two main areas in your answer:

– **language**: content, style and organisation
– **presentational devices**: photos, graphics, bullet points, colour, etc.

Autobiographies

- You may be given an extract from some **travel writing**, or an account of someone's life (**biography/autobiography**).

- This kind of non-fiction does not use presentational devices, so your focus must be on the **language**.

- Sometimes the text is **telling a story**, so think about the way the story builds up, and what the characters say and do.

This extract is from an **autobiography** by Sir Robin Day. Sir Robin used to interview politicians on television. Here, he describes his first ever time in front of the cameras. This was in the 1950s, when television was not so hi-tech!

Short sentences at start – makes the story dramatic.

Building tension – he is sweating from anxiety as well as heat.

Spoken dialogue, as in a story – adds interest and variety.

Countdown – adds tension.

> I was ready to go. But there was a little more delay. The lighting was causing trouble with my spectacles – reflection flashes from the lenses and shadows from the heavy hornrims. An engineer climbed up ladders to adjust the arc-lamps until the director in the control room was satisfied. It seemed to take a very long time. I began to sweat under the heat of the lights.
>
> We had been asked to memorise our material so that we would not have to look down. They wanted to see us looking full-face into the camera. I took a final look at my notes. The phrases which last night were crisp and bright seemed limp and dull, but it was too late to make any changes.
>
> 'Are you ready?' called the floor manager. I nodded.
>
> 'Stand by.' He stood to one side of the camera, and raised his arm above his shoulder.
>
> 'Thirty seconds to go ... Fifteen seconds.'
>
> Suddenly the floor-manager jabbed his hand down towards me. A red light glowed on top of the camera. This was it.

Describing detail – brings scene to life.

effective language – contrast of 'crisp and bright', then 'limp and dull'

short sentence – dramatic ending

Here is one way to start analysing the language used in the extract:

Robin Day is describing what he had to cope with when he presented a TV programme. He writes in a dramatic way. For example, he begins with a short sentence, which makes it seem tense, as if he is taking short breaths ...

The problems with the glasses and the lights are mentioned to show how everything seems to be going wrong, making Sir Robin more worried (he says 'I began to sweat ...', which isn't just from the heat in the studio). He tries to remember his lines, but 'The phrases ... seemed limp and dull'. Obviously, it is all building up inside him, and he thinks there is going to be a disaster. The countdown adds to the tension. The final short sentence is like a 'lift-off'. It makes you want to read on to see if it was OK.

Grade C

Good Points

- The student analyses in detail how the writer tells a good story.
- The use of language is always central to the answer.
- The purpose of this part of the text is taken into account.
- Relevant quotations are used to support the ideas.

Task

Write two paragraphs analysing the newspaper report on page 21. Comment on:

- the language
- the image and presentational devices.

Comparing texts

Key points

- One question will probably ask you to **compare two texts**. This means saying what is **similar** and/or **different** about the texts.

- The question should make it clear **which features of the texts are to be compared**.

- You need to **refer to both texts** in your answer, and link the texts.

Providing the right details

- Read the question carefully to make sure that you provide the **right information**. The wording of the question will show you exactly what you should be comparing in the texts. For example:

Which text is more successful?
Compare the texts by writing about how the writers have used:
  - fact and opinion
  - argument.

The **main question**, which asks you to compare the texts. The focus of your answer should be on how **successful** they are.

The **bullet points** list the particular features you must analyse – the writers' use of fact and opinion, and argument. You need to comment on how successful these features are, and say which works better in each text, and why.

Organising your answer

- You could discuss Text 1, then Text 2, and sum up how they are similar and/or different at the end, in a final paragraph. This is a straightforward approach, but it doesn't allow you to compare the texts until the end of your answer.

- Better is to take each point (bullet point) at a time, and compare both texts together.

- Begin a new paragraph each time you deal with a new point.

- End with a short paragraph that sums up your answer.

For example, you could structure your answer to the question above like this:

Para 1 - short introduction covering both texts, e.g. their purpose and audience
Para 2 - discuss use of fact and opinion in Text 1 and Text 2
Para 3 - discuss use of argument in Text 1 and Text 2
Para 4 - short conclusion referring back to main question: which text is more successful?

Linking the texts

- When you refer to the texts, you must clearly **link one text to the other**. This means using a linking word or phrase, e.g.

  The first text concentrates on giving advice to old people. <u>However</u>, the second text …

- Use some of the words and phrases on the right to make your comparisons clear:

when texts are similar	when texts are different
similarly	in contrast
just as … , so …	whereas
likewise	on the other hand
also	but
	however

Two texts to compare

> Compare these texts.
> Write about:
> - how they appeal to their audience
> - the use of language.

Text 1

This is from a teachers' newspaper. It is about an old teacher called Charles Crossley, describing his life and achievements.

> In his first teaching post at Loveridge Primary School, Crossley discovered by accident the power of poetry to keep unruly eight and nine-year-olds in order.
>
> 'I used to have a huge class of 50 or 60 boys every Friday afternoon,' he said. 'I was never properly prepared for the lesson, and they used to turn me into a nervous wreck. One Friday I opened a book of my poems in desperation and just read to them.'
>
> The boys were transfixed, and from then on were putty in his hands. 'They simply seemed to love the experience,' he said.

Text 2

This article from a local newspaper offers a different view of young people.

> ## Pensioner's life made a misery by 'young vandals'
>
> Frank Blackburn, 78, who lives on the Albany Estate, has been a prisoner in his house each evening for over a year. Groups of children, many as young as 7 or 8, have made him fear for his life and the safety of his property.
>
> ### Gangs
>
> Stones have been thrown through his windows, excrement has been pushed through his letter box and he cannot sleep. Gangs roam the area, shouting and drinking. Other older residents are just as fearful.
>
> 'The thugs gather every night,' says Frank. 'The police don't do anything about it.'

You could begin your answer like this:

Grade C

Begins by giving a general statement about the language in the extracts.

A personal response – if you can back up your opinion, this will gain you extra marks.

'however' makes a clear comparison with the first text.

> The language of the two texts is very different. In the first extract the language makes Crossley seems like an inspiring teacher: 'he discovered ... the power'. It is even a bit exaggerated – I can't imagine the boys being 'transfixed' and like putty, though it was the old days. In the second text, however, the language is unpleasant: 'misery', 'thugs'. Frank is a 'prisoner' in his own house. The estate is rough, full of 'stones', 'excrement', 'gangs' and fear. The final statement from Frank is that the police do nothing. This makes us sympathise with the old people even more.
>
> This difference is partly because the first article is looking back over someone's life and celebrating it, so the language is blown up a bit to make the teacher seem wonderful. Other teachers will like reading about this. Whereas the description of the estate in the other article is very upsetting and modern – which is what the writer intended.

This shows that the student is focusing on one extract first.

This shows that the student is now moving on to talk about the second text.

Brief quotations are used which are relevant to the points being made.

In this paragraph the student looks at the two texts together, and gives a reason why their language is different.

Task

Compare the two texts above by writing about their use of fact and opinion. Refer to the audience of each text in your answer.

Raising your grade

If you want to raise your grade to C or above, you need to show these skills.

Answer all parts of the question

- Read the question **carefully** and answer it **exactly**.

- If it asks you to comment on only part of a text, then don't comment on all of it.

- If it asks you to comment on the language used, then don't comment on the presentational devices.

- If **bullet point** 'prompts' are given, use them to structure your answer.

Show that you understand the text

- Think about the **type** of text that it is (biography? newspaper article? etc.) and refer to this in your answer.

- Think about **why** the text has been written (its **purpose**) and **who** it is written for (the **audience**).

- Talking about the text in this way shows that you **understand** it. For example:

  The writer seems to be addressing ordinary people. We know this because he uses short sentences and simple words. There are lots of illustrations, which would appeal to someone just glancing through the newspaper rather than spending ages reading it.

Comment on the text, don't just describe it

- The examiner doesn't want to know what is in the text, but about how **effects** are created.

- This means thinking about the **writer's techniques**, not just the content.

- Give **your opinion** about how effective you think certain features are.

  After lots of long sentences there is suddenly a short sentence, 'No good'. ✗

  After lots of long sentences there is suddenly a short sentence: 'No good'. <u>This shows how the runaway has come to the end of the road and has nowhere to turn. The reader stops, just like he does.</u> ✔

Refer to the texts in your answer

- Give **evidence** for your ideas by **quoting** from the text.

- Choose **brief** quotations and make sure they are **relevant** to the point you are making.

- Quote the words **exactly**, and put them in **inverted commas** ('…'). Or refer to the text by **summarising**.

- Give a **comment** which explains why you are quoting from the text.

  The writer presents himself as a pathetic figure: <u>he 'waves feebly at the taxi then steps away quickly as it races past him, covering him with muddy water'.</u> ✗

  The writer presents himself as a pathetic figure who <u>'waves feebly' at the taxi then gets splashed as it races past him.</u> This makes us laugh at him, but also feel a bit sorry for him.

Read the question and the student's answer below. The notes show why the examiner awarded it a C grade.

> What impression of Nivea for Men is this advertisement trying to create?
> In your answer, explain:
> - the use of language
> - the use of layout and presentational devices.

**BDF ●●●●
Beiersdorf**

THEY'VE RUN OUT OF HALF-TIME PIES.

**Life has enough irritations. Don't let your skin be one of them.
NIVEA FOR MEN® Extra Soothing Moisturiser soothes and calms your skin.**

Grade C

The advertisement is funny because it's advertising some products for skin care but the eye-catching writing makes you think it could be about pies. So the idea is that you want to know what on earth this has got to do with anything. And of course it fits the reader who is a man because they will know all about watching the match and not being able to get pies at half time.

The smaller writing at the bottom explains what it's all about. The 'irritation' joke is a good one because there are two meanings of irritation being used, skin irritation and annoyance. Humour is a good way of selling something. Also, the advertiser talks directly to the user – 'your skin'. This is another good technique because it makes the reader think they are being targeted.

The capitals look strong and manly like the person buying the product. Capitals are used for the name of the product at the bottom as well – in that case, because it's important. Otherwise it's interesting that the actual name of the product doesn't take up much space – though it's on the picture of the cream of course, so that we recognise it.

Most of the advertisement is blue, and blue is 'for a boy', so this is appropriate for men. The actual product is shown on the right of the advert. It looks straightforward, not flashy, and again, this will appeal to an average man who might not want to buy a beauty product.

Annotations:

The student shows an awareness of how the audience is being targeted.

Comments on the effect of the techniques.

Student moves on here to discuss the design features – s/he has used the bullet points in the question well to structure the answer. This helps the student to answer all parts of the question.

Tries to show an understanding of the main feature of the advert, though the expression is a bit unclear.

Good reference to the text – the student doesn't have to quote all the text but just puts the key word in inverted commas.

Another thoughtful comment – the student isn't just describing the text.

Another reference to the purpose and audience of the text.

Paper 2 Section A: Reading poems from different cultures and traditions

Key points

- Paper 2 Section A will focus on poems from different cultures and traditions. You have been reading these poems from your Anthology in class.

- There will be two questions, but you will only have to answer one of them. The question will ask you to compare one named poem with another poem of your choice.

- One question will target the first eight poems in the Anthology – Cluster 1. The other question will target the second eight poems – Cluster 2.

- This section of the exam counts for 15% of your total mark.

- You will spend about 45 minutes on your answer.

Top Tip!

Focus on your reading skills when answering the Reading questions. You won't get any marks for your spelling, punctuation and grammar.

The exam paper

Paper 2 has two sections. Section A is Reading Poetry. Section B is Writing to inform, explain, describe. Only Section A of the exam paper is given here.

Question 1 focuses on the 1st Cluster of poems in the Anthology. One poem is named and you choose another one to compare it with.

Question 2 focuses on the 2nd Cluster of poems in the Anthology. One poem is named and you choose another one to compare it with.

Paper 1 Section A: Foundation Tier

READING: POEMS FROM DIFFERENT CULTURES AND TRADITIONS

Answer one question.

You are allowed to refer to a copy of the Anthology in the examination.

EITHER

1 Compare *Night of the Scorpion* with any other poem of your choice. How do the poets present relationships in the poems?

Remember to:

- compare the poems
- write about relationships in the poems
- say how the relationships have been presented. *(27 marks)*

OR

2 How is language used to reveal the speaker's situation in *Not My Business* and in any other poem of your choice?

Remember to:

- write about the language used in the poems
- write about the speakers' situations
- deal with two poems. *(27 marks)*

You are given two questions, and you have to answer one of them.

You will be given a clean copy of the Anthology in the exam. You can't refer to your own marked-up copy.

The bullet points list the things you must write about. Make sure you cover all these in your answer.

The skills you will be assessed on

The questions that you are asked in Paper 2 Section A test certain reading skills. This table outlines the skills that are tested (on the left), and explains what you have to do to get good marks (on the right).

The skill you need to show

1 Understanding what the texts are about

Pages 30–47 ➤

2 Referring to the texts in your answer

Pages 30–47 ➤

3 Understanding the techniques that writers use

Pages 36–47 ➤

4 Choosing the right information and comparing texts

Pages 32–47 ➤

How to get good marks

- Know and explain **what the poems are about**.
- Think about the **meaning** of the poem. Often there are **deeper meanings** hiding under the obvious meaning.
- Understand **why** the poems have been written. What is the **purpose** of the poet in writing it?

- **Refer to the poems** in your answer, to provide evidence for your views.
- This includes the use of **quotations**.
- The references to the poems must be **relevant** to the point you are making.

- Show where the writers have used language to **create an effect**, e.g. powerful words or images.
- Explain **why** these techniques have been used, and **how effective** they are.
- Write about the **structure** of the poem, such as how it begins, develops and ends.
- Describe the **way it is set out on the page**, e.g. the lengths of the lines or stanzas (verses).

- **Select the right information** from the poems to answer the question, e.g. by skimming or scanning.
- Write about the ways in which the poems are **similar or different**.
- **Refer to examples** across both poems.

Question

It always helps to revise poems in pairs, since you have to compare two poems in the exam itself. Look at these lists. Which two poems from the list on the right would you use to answer each question, and why?

Question	Poems
A question about suffering	*Nothing's Changed*
A question about poverty	*Limbo*
A question about inequality	*Island Man*
A question about Man and Nature	*Night of the Scorpion*
A question about contrasting cultures	*What Were They Like?*
	Two Scavengers in a Truck…
	Blessing
	Vultures

Different cultures and traditions

Key points

- The poems in the Anthology all deal with **different cultures or traditions**.

- **Culture** refers to the ideas, beliefs and way of life of a particular race, country, religion or social group.

- **Traditions** are the customs that are commonly followed by people in a culture.

- The cultures and traditions are revealed by the **language** that is used, the **setting**, the **people**, and their **situations** and **problems**.

- You need to show that you **understand how** the poems reflect these different cultures and traditions.

Language

- In all the Anthology poems, language plays a big part in setting the poem within a particular culture.

  - It can show how people speak:

    munay hutoo kay aakhee jeebh aakhee bhasha

    (*from Search For My Tongue* by Sujata Bhatt)

    Explain yuself
    wha yu mean

    (*Half-Caste* by John Agard)

  - It gives us names: Oya, Shango and Hattie (*Hurricane Hits England*).

  - It mentions items unfamiliar to many people in Britain, e.g. yams in *Not My Business*; a salwar kameez in *Presents from my Aunts in Pakistan*; paddies and water buffalo in *What Were They Like?*

- It is very important to show that you understand **how** the poets use language, and **why**.

Look at this extract from a Grade C answer about the language used in *from Unrelated Incidents*.

Describes what the poem is doing.

Explains the poet's use of language.

Gives an example from the poem to back up the point.

The comment shows exactly how the use of language creates an effect.

In 'from Unrelated Incidents', Tom Leonard is criticising BBC English and all it represents. He does this by using a Scottish accent – the words are spelt in this accent to show they are spoken differently, for example 'wia' instead of 'with a'. This makes the newsreader seem like an ordinary person, not someone with a posh accent. Even though the newsreader suggests that Scottish people are rough ('wanna yoo scruff'), we wonder whether they are more honest than people who put on an accent like on the BBC.

Shows the reaction of the readers to the use of language.

Grade C

thi reason
a talk wia
BBC accent
iz coz yi
widny wahnt
mi ti talk
aboot thi
trooth wia
voice lik
wanna yoo
scruff...
yooz doant no
thi trooth
yirsellz cawz
yi canny talk
right.
(*from Unrelated Incidents*)

People and settings

The poets might write about people and places that are different from those we find in Britain. For example:

peasants; their life
was in rice and bamboo.

    (*What Were They Like?* by Denise Levertov)

a bright yellow garbage truck
  with two garbagemen in red plastic blazers
standing on the back stoop...

    (*Two Scavengers in a Truck, Two Beautiful People in a Mercedes* by Lawrence Ferlinghetti)

This poem is set in America. It is closer to our own world, but still different.

> **Top Tip!**
>
> When revising the poems, note the key words which tell the reader what is special or different about the people, the place or their beliefs.
> You can quote these words if they are relevant to the question you are answering.
> The key words are underlined in the examples on this page.

Situations and problems

The poets often write about problems that come from being in a different culture:

- **Being away from home**

  In *Island Man*, by Grace Nichols, the central character has left his island home and is now coping with life in a huge city. He has to drag himself out of bed to face the day:

  island man heaves himself
  Another London day

  The phrase 'another London day' makes his life seem heavy and depressing.

- **Slavery**

  In *Limbo*, Kamau Brathwaite describes the terrible suffering of the African slaves:

      stick is the whip
    and the dark deck is slavery

  The ending, though, suggests there might be hope of some kind:

      and the music is saving me.

- **Endless evil**

  Some poems are very dark, and seem to offer no hope:

  Vultures, by Chinua Achebe, is about 'the perpetuity of evil' – there is always going to be evil in the world, because of human nature.

  Nothing's Changed, by Tatamkhula Afrika argues that there are still divisions between blacks and whites in South Africa.

- **The struggle for existence**

  In many poems, people just have to struggle on:

  In *Night of the Scorpion*, Nissim Ezekiel describes his mother's suffering. The neighbours cannot help her, but rely on prayer and superstition.

- **Hope for the future**

  Sometimes there are some flashes of hope:

  In *This room*, Imtiaz Dharker describes a sense of joy and excitement:

  This is the time and place
  to be alive.

Task

Compare the way of life presented in *Two Scavengers from a Truck, Two Beautiful People in a Mercedes* with the way of life presented in any other poem of your choice from the Anthology.

Write about:
- what we learn of the people
- the kind of society in which they live
- how language is used by the poets.

Content, message and attitude

- When you write about poems from different cultures and traditions, you may have to comment on:
  - the **content** of the poems
  - the **messages** in the poems
  - the poets' **attitudes** to the subject.

What the poem is saying

- For each of the poems you are studying, you need to understand exactly **what the poem is about**. Ask yourself these questions: who? what? where? when? why?

These notes on the opening of *Vultures* by Chinua Achebe pick out the basic facts – what is going on in the poem.

A dawn scene is described.	In the greyness and drizzle of one despondent dawn unstirred by harbingers of sunbreak a vulture
A vulture sits in a tree.	perching high on broken bone of a dead tree
The vulture nestles up to his mate. Its physical appearance is described.	nestled close to his mate his smooth bashed-in head, a pebble on a stem rooted in a dump of gross feathers, inclined affectionately to hers. Yesterday they picked the eyes of a swollen corpse in a water-logged trench and ate the
They ate a corpse earlier on.	things in its bowel. Full gorged they chose their roost keeping the hallowed remnant
They sit on a branch after eating and watch the remains.	in easy range of cold telescopic eyes...

Top Tip!

When you write about a poem, you need to go deeper than the obvious surface meaning. Often the language will give you a clue as to the poet's meaning. For example:

The tree is 'dead' and the branch is described as a 'broken bone'. These are both images of death, which suit the fact that vultures are being described. The poet is telling us from the start that he is talking about death.

Going deeper: the meaning of the poem

- On a second reading of the poem, try to go deeper than understanding the bare facts. What **meaning** does the poet give to the bare details?

- Look closely at the **language** and **tone**. They give some clues to the meaning.

Here is the opening of *Vultures* again. This time the comments show the **meaning** of the individual details.

In the greyness and drizzle of one despondent dawn unstirred by harbingers of sunbreak a vulture	It's a depressing scene, which sets the tone for the poem.
perching high on broken bone of a dead tree	'broken bone' and 'dead tree' are images of death.
nestled close to his mate his smooth bashed-in head, a pebble on a stem rooted in a dump of gross feathers, inclined affectionately to hers. Yesterday they picked the eyes of a swollen corpse in a water-logged	The 'affection' is surprising for birds described as so ugly.
trench and ate the things in its bowel. Full gorged they chose their roost keeping the hallowed remnant in easy range of cold	Gruesome details – we feel disgusted.
telescopic eyes...	The description of their eyes makes them seem hard and unfeeling.

The message of the poem

- Poems always have a **message**. This might be a general observation about life, or it might be about rights and wrongs.

- In these poems, the message is often about the different culture.

- The message is not given openly – instead we slowly come to understand it the more we read the poem.

- You can often work out the message by moving from the **specific example(s)** described in the poem to a **general statement**:

Poem	Specific example(s) from the poem	General statement/message
Vultures	• Vultures can love in the midst of death. • Concentration camp commandant is evil but kind to his child.	• It is strange how all creatures, including humans, are a mix of good and evil.
Island Man	• A man from the Caribbean wakes in London but has images from his homeland.	• People who move from one culture to another are often torn between the two places.
Nothing's Changed	• District Six in Cape Town – the division between whites and blacks.	• Even after the end of Apartheid, there is division between whites and blacks, rich and poor.
from Unrelated Incidents	• Newsreader is talking in a Scottish accent, explaining that this could make him sound unbelievable to those who speak more 'correct' English.	• When people speak in non-standard English they are looked down on, but actually speaking in a 'posh' accent is false.
Not My Business	• Three people are 'disappeared' by people in power – the speaker doesn't help them, but then he too is taken away.	• Unless people help others in a violent society, everyone will suffer.

Commenting on meaning and message

- Remember to refer to the **language** of the poem to back up your comments.

This is how you could analyse lines 1–29 of Vultures:

The vultures are described in detail by the poet. They are described as ugly to look at, the male with a 'bashed-in head'. They have 'cold telescopic' eyes, which makes them frightening. The whole scene is a bit depressing: 'drizzle' and 'despondent'.

This is because death is part of the description. Although the birds are affectionate to each other, they have been eating a corpse, including its bowel – horrible details which make them even more frightening.

The next section makes a general comment – the poet says it's strange how those in love can ignore horrible things around them. The idea of falling asleep in a 'charnel-house' is powerful, because a charnel-house is like an abattoir.

Grade C

Good Points

- The student goes beyond the factual meaning of the poem to discuss the underlying meaning.
- References to the language are used to show the meaning.
- All the ideas are supported with details from the text.
- There are three clear sections: the birds, their behaviour and the general point (the message).

READING POETRY

The poet's attitude to the subject

- You might be asked to comment on **the poet's own feelings** about the situation in the poems.

- You can often work out these feelings by studying the **language** the poet uses.

- These notes show how Niyi Osundare's attitude is clear from the start in *Not My Business*. We are shown what is happening in the society and how people react to it. People ignore the suffering of others and think only of themselves.

'stuffed' suggests rough treatment, 'belly' suggests they fed him to an animal or monster – another frightening image.

They picked Akanni up one morning
Beat him soft like clay
And stuffed him down the belly
Of a waiting jeep.
  What business of mine is it
  So long they don't take the yam
  From my savouring mouth?

The simile ('like clay') shows that Akanni was beaten to a pulp. This is reinforced by the word 'soft', which also implies he was powerless.

The speaker's actual words are quoted. It is clear that he doesn't want to be involved. 'Savouring' suggests that he is only worried about his own satisfaction.

However, the fact that the speaker has tried not to get involved does not save him. His turn comes too:

He is frozen with fear – just as others have been fearful.

And then one evening
As I sat down to eat my yam
A knock on the door froze my hungry hand.
The jeep was waiting on my bewildered lawn
Waiting, waiting in its usual silence.

He was more interested in his yams than in his neighbours' problems.

He is bewildered – how could this happen to him?

'usual silence' emphasises how everyone has been silent about the arrests.

- Sometimes the poet's attitude may be unclear, because he or she has mixed feelings. In *Vultures*, for example, the poet ends by saying:

    Praise bounteous providence …
(We could praise because there is love even in an ogre.)

    or else despair …
(We could despair because there is evil even in the 'germ' of love.)

We are left to make up our own minds.

Writing about attitude and message

- When you are writing about the poet's attitude or message you must **explain exactly what you mean**.
- You must also **support your comments** by referring closely to the poem.

In this example, a student was asked:
- to explain the poet's attitude to what happens in *Not My Business*
- to say what the reader can learn from the poem.

Grade C

Starts with a general comment about the subject of the poem and how it is structured. This is one of the ways the poet shows his attitude, by making a contrast.

From the start, the poem shows a contrast between someone being picked up by the police or the army, and then someone else saying how it is not their business. The three lines at the end of each stanza are from this other person who just stands by, doing nothing.

The poet makes it clear that there is suffering. For example, he uses names (Akanni, Danladi and Chinwe), which makes them seem like real people he knows. The detail also backs this up – Akanni, for instance, is beaten 'soft like clay', and when they come for Danladi, they 'booted the whole house awake'. The language is violent like the scene. There is also a mystery, for example Chinwe's job is taken for no clear reason and this is frightening.

Detail about how the language of the poem presents the poet's attitude: real people are involved, real violence, and frightening mystery.

Explains how we are meant to be sympathetic to the victims, and critical of the speaker for doing nothing.

So we are meant to be sympathetic to the people disappearing. But the other person continues to eat yams and look after himself. He is presented in a bad way, which is odd because he is the speaker in the poem, but we must remember that doesn't always mean he is the poet. In fact, it is clear that the poet is criticising him, as I have said.

In the end, the poet shows us that hoping to avoid trouble does not help anyone escape from oppression. This is the real message of the poem. He does this by showing how the speaker himself is picked up. The 'knock on the door' at the end is terrifying and even stops the speaker eating. This is where his silence led: to the jeep waiting on the lawn.

Explains the message of the poem.

Top Tip!

If you want to analyse the poet's attitude or message, ask yourself these questions:
- **What** is being said?
- **How** is it presented?
- **Why** is it presented in that way?

Question

Read *Blessing* by Imtiaz Dharker.
- What happens in the poem?
- What is the poet's attitude to it?
- What message can we take from the poem and in what way is it different from the message in *Not My Business*?

Structure

Key points

- You could be asked about the **structure** of the poems.

- This means analysing how each poem is **organised**: how it opens, develops and concludes.

- It also means analysing how each poem is **set out on the page**.

How the poem is organised

- Lawrence Ferlinghetti's *Two Scavengers in a Truck, Two Beautiful People in a Mercedes* could be broken into five sections:

  lines 1–9   a description of the truck and the Mercedes caught together at the stoplight

  lines 10–15   the 'elegant' couple in the Mercedes are described

  lines 16–25   the 'grungy' couple in the garbage truck are described

  lines 26–30   the 'scavengers' looking down at the couple

  lines 31–37   message: they are close yet far apart.

  Note how this structure helps to organise the poet's ideas. We are led from step to step, ending with the poet's thoughts (the message).

- In contrast, *Night of the Scorpion* by Nissim Ezekiel is a **narrative**. The poem describes what happens to Ezekiel's mother over 20 hours. It tells:

  - what the scorpion did

  - how the neighbours react

  - how the incident is given a religious significance (*May the poison purify your flesh*)

  - the father's efforts to cure her

  - what his mother says at the end.

Structural devices

The poems in the Anthology use a variety of **structural devices**.
Look out for these when you comment on structure:

- **refrain** – a repeated chorus

  The refrain in *Limbo* suggests a kind of performance, as in a limbo dance:

  limbo
  limbo like me

- **stanza** – a fixed number of lines arranged in a pattern

  In *Not My Business*, the stanzas break into two parts: the first four lines tell what is happening to others, the final three lines tell how the speaker is reacting:

  They came one night
  Booted the whole house awake
  And dragged Danladi out,
  Then off to a lengthy absence.
     What business of mine is it
     So long they don't take the yam
     From my savouring mouth?

- **repetition** – of words or phrases

  Half-Caste uses repetition to challenge the listener's or reader's views about 'half-castes':

  Explain yuself
  wha yu mean.

- **pattern** – a repeated movement that gives shape to the poem.

  Vultures has:

  – a stanza about the birds, followed by a stanza with a general statement about what this means.

  – a stanza about the Commandant, followed by a stanza with a general statement, which links the birds and the man.

How the poem is presented

- The **different line lengths and indentations** which are a feature of Lawrence Ferlinghetti's *Two Scavengers in a Truck, Two Beautiful People in a Mercedes* suggest the movement in the travellers' lives:

> At the stoplight waiting for the light
> > nine a.m. downtown San Francisco
> a bright yellow garbage truck
> > with two garbagemen in red plastic blazers
> standing on the back stoop
> > one on each side hanging on
> and looking down into
> > an elegant open Mercedes
> > with an elegant couple in it

> There is no punctuation at the end of lines, so the sentence runs on. The effect is to suggest this is a 'slice of life' that doesn't begin or end – it is endless.

- Later, the lines on the page may even suggest the sea's movement:

> > across that small gulf
> > in the high seas
> > > of this democracy.

If you had to comment on the layout of this poem, you could write:

> The poem gives the impression of someone speaking. Their pauses might be the breaks in the lines. It looks random, but sometimes the position of the words on the lines makes sense:
> > 'and looking down into
> > > an elegant open Mercedes
> > > with an elegant couple in it'.
> In this extract the reader's eye drops to the next line, like the garbagemen looking down at the car.

Note how the layout is **explained**, rather than just identified: 'The reader drops to the next line …'

- The layout of *Night of the Scorpion* is **solid blocks of text**. This suits a narrative poem. The mother's words are contained in their own short stanza at the end to emphasise their significance:

> My mother only said
> Thank God the scorpion picked on me
> and spared my children.

- The **shape of the lines** in *Limbo* conveys the movements of the limbo dancers:

> knees spread wide
> and the dark ground is under me
>
> down
> down
> down

Question

Read *What Were They Like?* by Denise Levertov.
- How is the poem structured?
- Why has it been structured in this way?
- How successful is this structure?

Language

- You will always have to write about the **language** in the poems.

- You need to comment on **poetic techniques** (e.g. similes, rhyme and rhythm) and **language use** (how the poet uses words, sentences and punctuation).

- You will also need to **explain what effect** the language has on the reader.

Poetic techniques

- **Similes** are comparisons using 'like' or 'as':

  The peasants came like swarms of flies
  (Night of the Scorpion)

  Comparing the peasants to flies makes them seem irritating, like pests.

- **Metaphors** are direct comparisons – giving something the qualities of something else:

  the bud opens, the bud opens in my mouth
  (from Search for My Tongue)

  The new tongue is described as a flower that blossoms in the speaker's mouth.

- **Symbols** are objects that stand for a general idea:

  In *from Search for My Tongue*, the idea of being caught between two languages and two cultures is symbolised by the two tongues that grow in the speaker's mouth.

- **Rhythm** is the beat of the poem – the pattern made by the sounds of the words:

  he always comes back   groggily groggily
  Comes back to sands
  (Island Man)

  The rhythm suggests the beating of the waves on the shore.

- **Rhyme** is when words end with the same sound. The words could be at the ends of lines (as below), or within the lines:

  when the daily furniture of our lives
  stirs, when the improbable arrives.
  (This room)

  The rhyme emphasises those words.

- **Repetition** means using the same words or groups of words:

  but yu must come back tomorrow
  wid de whole of yu eye
  an de whole of yu ear
  an de whole of yu mind
  (Half-Caste)

  The repetition emphasises how people who say 'half-caste' are not looking at the whole picture.

- **Alliteration** is when words that are close together begin with the same letter:

  Brash with glass,
  name flaring like a flag
  (Nothing's Changed)

  The repeated 'fl' sound emphasises the name of the whites only inn, as if it is fluttering in the speaker's face.

- **Assonance** is when the same vowel sounds are repeated:

> *What is the meaning of trees …*
> *Their cratered graves?*
> > *(Hurricane Hits England)*

The 'ee' sound is repeated in the first line, and the 'ay' sound in the second line. These sounds may suggest the sounds of the hurricane.

- Sometimes the sound of the words represents the sound of the action being described (this is called **onomatopoeia**):

> *Imagine the drip of it,*
> *the small splash, echo*
> *in a tin mug*
> > *(Blessing)*

The poet represents the drip and the splash by the words she uses.

- You need to do more than just **name** the poetic techniques. The examiner is looking for an **explanation** of why they have been used and the **effect** they are creating.

And limbo stick is the silence in front of me *limbo*	*limbo* *limbo like me*
limbo *limbo like me* *limbo* *limbo like me*	long dark deck and the water surrounding me long dark deck and the silence is over me
long dark night is the silence in front of me *limbo* *limbo like me*	*limbo* *limbo like me*
stick hit sound and the ship like it ready	stick is the whip and the dark deck is slavery
stick hit sound and the dark still steady	stick is the whip and the dark deck is slavery
	limbo *limbo like me*
	drum stick knock and the darkness is over me

If you were analysing the poetic techniques used in *Limbo*, you could write this:

'Limbo' is an attempt to show the suffering of the African slaves as they are transported to America. So the rhyme and rhythm of the poem suggests the limbo dance, and maybe also the slaves dancing and chanting on the ship. For example, there is a repeated 'chorus', like the chorus of a song:

> 'limbo
> limbo like me'.

The repetition in the poem adds to the effect of a dance or song, such as 'and the ship like it ready … and the dark still steady'. You can almost imagine the slaves stamping their feet – or the audience clapping the limbo dancers.

The poem is also very symbolic. The 'stick' is a limbo stick, but also represents the way in which the slaves are beaten. The stick is their master. The 'dark deck' stands for their slavery, the darkness shows that light and joy have gone from their lives. The alliteration of 'd's emphasises this idea.

Grade C

Describes the purpose of the poem and links it to techniques. All poetic effects have a purpose.

Gives an example, and explains that it is used to suggest a song.

Names the technique (repetition), gives an example, and explains its effect.

Names the technique (symbolism) and gives a detailed example.

READING POETRY

Other language use

You need to identify where particular **words**, **sentences** or **punctuation** (commas, full stops, etc.) have been used for effect. These language features will have been chosen by the poet to give meaning to the poem.

- Individual words might create a **particular effect**:

  My mother cherished her jewellery –
  Indian gold, dangling, filigree.
      (Presents from my Aunts in Pakistan)

  The detailed description of the jewellery, especially the unusual word 'filigree', makes it seem foreign and fascinating.

- Some words may have **associations**, making the reader think of something else, which adds meaning:

  fumes of human roast
      (Vultures)

  'Roast' suggests a meal, which makes the image of human death even more disgusting. It also links back to the vultures' meal.

- Note the **length of the sentences**:

  In *Blessing* by Imtiaz Dharker, the sentences get longer and longer. This contrasts the dryness of drought with the flood of water when the pipe bursts.

- Look closely at the **punctuation** as well:

  Island Man has no punctuation other than capital letters. This suggests the dreamlike state the man is in.

- The **position** of the words on the line can be important:

  This is the time and place
  to be alive
      (This room)

  Putting 'to be alive' on its own line suggests this is a key idea in the poem.

- These notes show how Derek Walcott has used language in *Love After Love*:

Love After Love

The time will come
When, with elation,
You will greet yourself arriving
At your own door, in your own mirror,
And each will smile at the other's welcome,

And say sit here. Eat.
You will love again the stranger who was your self.
Give wine. Give bread. Give back your heart
To itself, to the stranger who has loved you

All your life, whom you ignored
For another, who knows you by heart.
Take down the love-letters from the bookshelf

The photographs, the desperate notes,
Peel your own images from the mirror.
Sit. Feast on your life.

'own' is repeated to emphasise 'yourself'. (Central idea of poem is coming to terms with yourself.)

Simple language (with repetition of 'and') emphasises the peace and simplicity of the action.

List of what must be done to love again: sentences begin with commands, e.g. 'take', 'peel'.

Emphasises joy from the start. Commas make you pause, to highlight the feeling.

Simple pleasure shown by one-word sentence.

Wine and bread have religious (Christian) meaning.

Repetition of 'heart' – appropriate in a love poem.

Sentences get shorter as the old complicated life becomes simpler.

Idea of celebrating, enjoying life again – 'Feast' refers back to wine and bread earlier.

Analysing the language use

- When you discuss the way the poet uses language:

  1 Make a **point**, e.g. *The poet describes the slippers in detail.*

  2 Refer to the **evidence**, e.g. *'embossed slippers, gold and black points curling'*

  3 Comment on the **effect** of the language, e.g. *The texture (embossed) and the colour show how unusual and special they are.*

Top Tip!

Remember PEE:
- Point
- Evidence
- Effect

If you had to analyse the use of language in *Love After Love*, you could begin like this:

Overall purpose of the poem given, to give context for the detailed comments that follow.

Language use identified (short sentence), and its purpose commented on.

> *Walcott is writing a poem to show that coming to terms with ourselves and who we really are brings peace. From the beginning, he focuses on happiness – the strong word 'elation' makes this clear, and 'smile' and 'welcome' support it. He stresses that we are in our 'own' place and can enjoy the experience.*
>
> *He describes us returning to simple pleasures. 'Eat' is a one-word sentence, at the end of the line. This makes it important – perhaps Walcott is saying that we can feed ourselves, we do not need others. The mention of wine and bread, with their religious significance, makes the eating almost religious. Later in the poem this image of feasting is used again ('Feast on your life'). He is saying that we have enough memories and knowledge to feed us as long as we live.*

Grade C

Examples given to support purpose given. Brief reference to text.

Language use identified (image of feasting), and its effect and purpose commented on. Brief reference to the text.

Comparing language use

- When you compare two poems, part of your answer is likely to compare the way the poets use language.

Look at how language is used in these two extracts. The overall mood of the poems is very different – how does the language help to convey that mood?

'I' used a lot for emphasis

Words suggest hatching.

Sentence runs on over the ends of the lines – suggests movement.

Words suggest upward movement.

also movement from dark to light

> This room is breaking out
> of itself, cracking through
> its own walls
> in search of space, light,
> empty air.
> The bed is lifting out of
> its nightmares.
> From dark corners, chairs
> are rising up to crash through clouds.
>
> *This room* by Imtiaz Dharker

list

sound effects

> I tried each satin-silken top –
>   was alien in the sitting-room.
> I could never be as lovely
>   as those clothes –
>   I longed
> for denim and corduroy.
>   My costume clung to me
>   and I was aflame,
> I couldn't rise up out of its fire,
>   half-English,
>   unlike Aunt Jamila.
>
> *Presents from my Aunts in Pakistan*
>   by Moniza Alvi

Alliteration emphasises the quality of the top.

Powerful word – shows feelings of speaker.

Simile – she compares herself to the clothes.

Alliteration emphasises the suffocation.

Metaphor – she is being burnt up.

Suggests image of the phoenix – but she can't be reborn (as the phoenix was).

Task

Compare the use of language in *This room* and *Presents from my Aunts in Pakistan*. Include some of the points given above.

Comparing two poems

Key points

- Paper 2 Section A will ask you to **compare two poems**.

- The question will highlight **what aspects** of the poems you need to compare. This comparison must be the focus of your answer.

- Begin with a brief **introduction** and sum up with a **conclusion**.

- Support your views with **clear references** to the poems.

Reading the question

One poem is always named; you choose the poem to compare it with.

Compare *Nothing's Changed* with another poem from a different culture or tradition. Show how the people in the poems react to their surroundings. You should write about:
- the ideas in the poems
- the poets' attitudes to the situations they describe
- how the poets use language to show you these things.

Focus your comparison on this point. Don't compare the two poems in general terms.

The bullet points outline what you should write about.

Planning your answer

- When you have chosen which question to answer, and which poem you are going to compare with the named poem, spend five minutes planning your answer.

- Jot down ideas about each poem in turn. Use the bullet points in the question to organise these ideas. For example:

> Island Man
>
> <u>ideas</u>
>
> seems at home at first
> gradually he comes back to reality - London
> he can imagine a better life but
> he accepts his situation
>
> <u>poet's attitude</u>
>
> she stresses wonder of life in Caribbean
> seems torn between two worlds - accepts both?
> last line suggests being in London is a drag
>
> <u>language</u>
>
> sound effects - suggests waves of sea
> vivid setting and detail
> 'groggily groggily' - doesn't want to wake
> 'heaves' - unwilling

Top Tip!

When you choose the second poem, make sure it will let you make good comparisons in the areas outlined in the question. (In the answers on pages 44–45, the student has chosen to compare *Nothing's Changed* with *Island Man*.)

Top Tip!

The bullet points in the question are very useful. They show you exactly what you should write about.
- Use them to brainstorm ideas when you plan your answer.
- Use them to structure your answer, by writing a paragraph on each bullet point.

Referring to the poems

- Make sure that you refer to **both poems** in your answer.

- Refer to **relevant details**. Keep the focus of the question in mind.

- You should **compare the texts**. Don't just write about one, then the other, without saying how they are similar or different.

- When referring to the texts, **link one text to the other**. Words and phrases such as 'however', 'similarly', 'in contrast', 'on the other hand' are useful when you do this.

Page 24

Using quotations and examples

- Always support your ideas by referring to the poems. There are different ways of doing this:

  – Refer to the poem **without quoting directly**:

> Agard goes on to consider whether music is half-caste as well. He refers to the composer Tchaikovsky mixing black and white keys on the piano – which of course he had to do to produce a symphony.

  – **Include brief quotations** from the poem. Quote the exact words and put them inside inverted commas:

> Tom Leonard's words are spelt as they are spoken by someone with a strong Scottish accent, for example 'wanna you scruff' and 'yi canny talk right'.

  – If you are **referring to a longer passage**, or you are quoting two or more lines of the poem, set the passage out on a new line, after a colon:

> The language used to describe water cleverly portrays the sound of the water:
>
> 'Imagine the drip of it,
> the small splash, echo
> in a tin mug'

Top Tip!

Don't waste time by copying out long quotations. When you are commenting on longer passages, it's better to write about them than to copy out chunks of text.

READING POETRY

Writing the introduction

- Begin your answer with a brief introduction (one paragraph).

- Introduce both poems and relate them to the subject of the question.

You could write an **opening paragraph** to the question on page 42 like this:

Grade C

First poem summarised briefly.

Further detail refers to the focus of the question (how the man reacts to the situation).

Further detail refers to the focus of the question (the situation in the poem).

Second poem summarised briefly, and a clear comparison made.

> In 'Nothing's Changed', we have a picture of South Africa after the end of apartheid. The poet is suggesting that life has not improved, and has produced a protest poem which shows the unfairness in that country. The situation in 'Island Man' is different, because Grace Nichols reveals how a Caribbean island man still thinks of his home, but has to get up and cope with existence in London where he has moved. He may not be happy, but has chosen this way of living.

Top Tip!

Make sure your opening paragraph:
- refers to both poems
- refers to the focus of the question
- is brief and clear.

Good Points

- The student **focuses on the question**.
- The poems are **summarised briefly**.
- From the start, the student **compares the poems**.

Writing the main part of the answer

- In the main part of your answer you should write a detailed comparison of the two poems. You could follow this plan:

  1 Write in detail about one poem, using the bullet points in the question to organise your paragraphs.

  2 Then write in detail about the other poem, again using the bullet points.

  3 When discussing the second poem, refer back to the first where appropriate to make your comparisons.

You could write a **detailed comparison**, as below:

(Note: in the following answer, the student has already written about *Nothing's Changed*. These paragraphs focus on the second poem, *Island Man*. Only the beginning of the detailed comparison is shown.)

Clear signal that the student is now turning to the second poem.

Backs up points by close reference to the text, and by giving comments on the passages quoted.

New paragraph for a new point, but focus is still on the second poem.

> When we examine 'Island Man', we see that his situation is similar in that he, too, can imagine a better life. In his case, though, it is a beautiful life he has known already. Details such as 'the sound of blue surf' and 'fishermen pushing out to sea' give a vivid picture of the sound and sights of the homeland he loves so much, brought out by the repeated 's' sounds, which suggest the sound of the sea.
>
> Island Man seems to accept his situation ('he always comes back...'), even though reluctantly, as suggested by the miserable last line 'Another London day'. This contrasts with the first poem, which can see no hope for black people in South Africa and where the speaker feels like turning to violence.

Grade C

Focus is on the 'better life' in the second poem, though a comparison is made with the first poem.

Cross-reference to the first poem to show comparison.

Writing the conclusion

- In a final paragraph, summarise the key points you have made.
- You could also make a comment on how successful you think the poems are.

You could write a **concluding paragraph** like this:

Sums up the first poem's message.

Sums up the second poem's viewpoint. The student gives an opinion about the poem's success ('very clear').

> The way people react to their surroundings, therefore, is treated very differently in each poem. Tatamkhulu Afrika thinks violence is the only answer: in the last stanza there is the image of a bomb smashing the glass. The last line, though, returns us to the start, because 'Nothing's changed' (which is the title of the poem). 'Island Man', however, seems resigned to his life, and leaves his dreams behind to start 'Another London day'. The contrast between his life as it was and his life as it is has been made very clear.

Grade C

'Therefore' signals a summing up. Note the student still has the focus of the question in mind.

Task

Show how *Half-Caste* and one other poem from a different culture present the feelings of people who do not feel part of the society around them.
Write about:

- the problems the people have
- their feelings
- how successfully their feelings are shown.

Raising your grade

If you want to raise your grade to C or above, you need to show these skills.

Refer to the poems effectively

- Make a **point** and back it up by **referring to** or **quoting from** the text.

> The scavengers, compared to the couple in the car, are ugly. The description 'gargoyle Quasimodo' shows this clearly by referring to two ugly images. ✔

- Choose **brief** quotations, and make sure they are **relevant** to the point you are making.

- Add a **comment** which explains why you are quoting from the text.

- Quote the words **exactly**, using **inverted commas** or **summarise** the text.

Make clear cross-references between poems

- Make sure you mention both poems in your **introduction**. Sum up their similarities and differences in your **conclusion**.

- When you discuss the second poem, **compare** it with the first whenever you can.

- Use words like '**whereas** in the first poem …' and 'in this poem, **however**, …' to show how you are comparing the poems.

> The lines are not divided into stanzas, so we seem to just follow her thoughts, whereas the second poem is much more organised, which shows … ✔

Show you are aware of the poets' techniques and purposes

- Don't just make comments on the effects of certain words or images. Go further and show that you are spotting a **deliberate technique** by the poet:

> The 'ice white glass, linen falls, single rose' is made to appear fragile and beautiful, which is <u>deliberately contrasted</u> with the world of the working blacks: 'wipe your fingers …' ✔

- Show in your comments that **you know why** the poet is using language in this way.

> The Gujerati script shows the problems of dealing with a foreign tongue. ✘

> The Gujerati script, even when translated, is alien to us. The poet is showing us how difficult it must be for the speaker to cope with two languages. ✔

Show you understand the poets' feelings, attitudes and ideas

- Don't just focus on the content. Discuss the **deeper meaning** and the **poets' attitude** to what they are describing. **Develop your comments** to show you really understand.

> The society we see in Two Scavengers is one that is in two parts. ✘

> The society we see in Two Scavengers is one that is in two parts. On one side there are the scavengers, and on the other … ✔

Read the question and an extract from the student's answer below.
This is only a practice task, but the notes show how it demonstrates Grade C qualities.

Compare how language has been used in the endings of *This room* and *Presents from my Aunts in Pakistan.*

This room

Pots and pans bang together
In celebration, clang
Past the crowd of garlic, onions, spices,
Fly by the ceiling fan.
No one is looking for the door.

In all this excitement
I'm wondering where
I've left my feet, and why

My hands are outside, clapping.

Presents from my Aunts in Pakistan

Sometimes I saw Lahore –
                        my aunts in shaded rooms,
screened from male visitors,
            sorting presents,
                        wrapping them in tissue.

Or there were beggars, sweeper-girls
            and I was there –
                        of no fixed nationality,
staring through fretwork
                        at the Shalimar Gardens.

Grade C

Effective reference to the poem: brief and relevant to the point being made.

Shows awareness of the poet's purpose.

Now discusses the second poem, but makes comparisons with the first poem.

The extract from 'This room' begins with a lot of noise – lots of 'p's and the sound of 'pans bang', followed by the rhyme 'clang'. There is even a 'crowd of garlic, onions, spices', an image which makes them sound like spectators somewhere. This list stretches through the first sentence of the stanza, and it could make you think this is frightening as it builds up, but the final sentence takes the worry away:
    'No one is looking for the door.'
    Dharker feels as if everything is suddenly out of her control, and the way the sentences run over the lines in the second stanza back this up. Though the final line, ending with 'clapping', shows that she is excited about it.
    'Presents from my Aunts in Pakistan' is much calmer. It begins with a rhyme, 'saw Lahore', which seems slow. The description of her aunts' existence is not full of movement like 'This room.' Instead words like 'shaded' and 'screened' describe how they are hidden quietly away. This world seems safer, but lacks the 'excitement' of Dharker's room.
    Alvi ends by describing herself as 'of no fixed nationality'. She is outside society. This is symbolised by the picture of her staring through the fretwork of the gates ...

Shows awareness of the poet's technique, and adds a comment on the quotation.

Understands what the poet is feeling, backed up by evidence from the poem.

Shows awareness of the poet's technique (symbol).

Paper 1 Section B and Paper 2 Section B: Writing

Key points

- Section B of both English papers tests your writing skills.

- In each paper you have to choose just one question.

- In Paper 1 you have to write to argue, persuade and/or advise. In Paper 2 you have to inform, explain and/or describe.

Pages 62–85

- Section B of Paper 1 counts for 15% of your total mark. Section B of Paper 2 counts for a further 15% of your total mark.

- You should spend about 45 minutes on each answer. That means writing between one and two sides of paper.

The exam paper

This is an example of Paper 1 Section B. Paper 2 Section B is organised in exactly the same way.

Each paper consists of two sections. Section A (not given here) is the Reading questions.

In Paper 1 Section B (here) you have to write to argue, persuade, advise. In Paper 2 Section B (not given here) you have to write to inform, explain, describe.

Paper 1 Section B: Foundation Tier

WRITING TO ARGUE, PERSUADE OR ADVISE

Answer **one** question.

You are advised to spend about 45 minutes on this section.

EITHER

3 Write an article for your local newspaper, **arguing** that there is too much pressure on teenagers and that they should be allowed to enjoy 'the best years of their lives'.

You might wish to write about:

- pressures at school
- pressures at home
- why being a teenager should be a happy time.

Remember to:

- write an article
- choose the right language to argue. *(27 marks)*

Choose one question only in Section B.

OR

4 Writing as a celebrity chef, produce a newspaper column to **persuade** parents to encourage their children to eat healthily.

You might wish to write about:

- why healthy eating is important
- what children should eat
- how parents can encourage children to eat healthily.

Remember to:

- write a persuasive newspaper column
- use the right language for parents
- focus on healthy eating. *(27 marks)*

Use the bullet points to help you plan your answer.

The skills you will be tested on

The questions in Section B of each paper are designed to test your writing skills. This table outlines the skills that are tested, and explains what you have to do to get good marks.

The skill you need to show	How to get good marks
1 Communicate clearly and imaginatively *Pages 50–51 and 62–85*	• Think of ideas that are **relevant** to the question, and present them **clearly**. • Make your answer **varied** and **imaginative** so that it keeps the reader's interest.
2 Write for different readers and purposes *Pages 50–51 and 62–85*	• You must know how to write for a specific **purpose** (e.g. to advise) and how to write in a specific **form** (e.g. a letter). • You also need to know how to target a specific **audience** (e.g. younger people).
3 Organise your ideas *Pages 52–53*	• Give your ideas some kind of **structure**. • Write a good **opening**, a clear **sequence of paragraphs** for the main section and a powerful **conclusion**. • Write in **paragraphs** and **vary the length** of the paragraphs for effect.
4 Write in sentences *Pages 54–55*	• Your writing must **make sense**. • Make sure your sentences are **varied and effective** and that they suit the type of writing. • Write sentences of **different lengths**. • Write sentences of **different types** (e.g. questions, commands, statements).
5 Use a wide vocabulary *Pages 56–57*	• Use words that suit the **purpose** and **audience** of your writing. • Try to use **interesting** and **powerful** words. • **Vary** your words and avoid repetition. • Use **techniques** such as imagery, repetition and contrasts, where they suit the type of writing.
6 Punctuate your sentences accurately *Pages 58–59*	• Make sure each sentence begins with a **capital letter** and ends with a **full stop**. • Use a **wider range** of punctuation where you can, such as commas, apostrophes, exclamation marks, question marks and quotation marks.
7 Spell accurately *Pages 60–61*	• You need to know how to **spell words you use regularly**. • Apply **spelling rules** whenever possible. • You will gain more marks if you can spell a wider range of words.

Ideas and planning

Key points

- You should spend **up to 10 minutes planning** your answer.

- First, **think of ideas** that you can use in your writing.

- When doing this, you should always keep in mind the **purpose** and **audience** of the task.

- Then **structure** your ideas and **develop** them.

Thinking of ideas: audience and purpose

- First, highlight the **key words** in the question title. These will help you identify the purpose and audience of the task.

- The **purpose** of your response will be to argue, persuade, advise, inform, explain or describe.

- The **audience** (the people you are writing for) may be of a certain age or from a certain background, e.g. children or school governors.

- The audience and purpose affect the **style** and **tone** of your writing (e.g. informal or formal, serious or funny), the **form** of your writing (e.g. a letter, speech or article), and its **content**.

This is how you could make notes on a question from Paper 1:

purpose: formal writing

Write a section for a school booklet to be sent to teachers applying for a job at your school. Offer them advice on how to cope with any problems they might encounter.

audience: will need clear but basic advice, since they will be just starting the job

purpose: to identify the problems and tell the new teachers exactly how they might cope with them

This is how you could make notes on a question from Paper 2:

purpose: explain, don't just inform

purpose: focus on activities away from school/work

Explain why you spend your free time in the way you do. Write about:
- the way you spend your evenings
- what you do at weekends
- why you find these activities interesting and worthwhile.

purpose: to give the reasons why you spend your time in these ways

Top Tip!

The questions in Paper 2 often don't say exactly who the audience is. If that happens, assume that you are writing for the examiner. Your style should be quite formal.

Structuring your ideas

- Put your ideas together, first of all as **brief notes**.

- You could produce your ideas as a **spider diagram**:

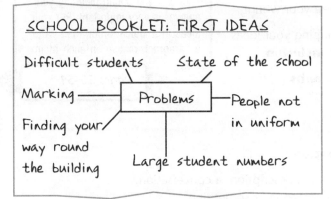

SCHOOL BOOKLET: FIRST IDEAS

Difficult students   State of the school

Marking —— Problems —— People not
                                        in uniform
Finding your
way round
the building   Large student numbers

- Or you could **list them** in the order you might deal with them in your actual answer:

Free time
Evenings - homework, Tai Kwon Do, music,
X Box

Weekends - town, football matches,
cleaning (!), friends

Why - relaxation, fitness, self-improvement,
a change

Developing your ideas

- Now develop the basic ideas by adding **further detail** on your plan.

- Although planning time is short, you will benefit later. It will be easier to write the actual answer, because you will know **exactly what details to mention** in each section.

You could begin to **develop the ideas** for the school booklet like this.

School booklet

Difficult students:
Problems: aggressive to teachers -
regular fights - lots of exclusions
Advice: try listening and being
understanding; don't be too strict but
apply the rules

State of the school:
Problems: needs repairs - old desks -
leaking roof - vandalism
Advice: set an example by keeping your
classroom tidy/get any graffiti removed
that you see; set up after-school
litter patrols

Here's another example. The writing task is:
'Describe the person you most admire in the world.'

1 Uncle Frank: age, kind of person he is,
how others see him, why he's my hero -
story to explain this
2 How he found out about his illness. The
effect it had: job/home.
3 Aunty Jane's situation. What she said.
What they did. The outcome. Family
involvement.
4 What he's been like since, with other
people and on trips to the hospital.
5 Fundraising: his pain and his gains,
reports in local paper, award from
Queen
6 His future plans: ending with hope,
quote from Uncle

Good Points

- The notes are broken into sections. These could also show where you begin a new paragraph. Sometimes, you might want to turn one of the sections into two or three shorter paragraphs.
- There is a 'core idea' for each section, then further detail on what could be included.

Task

1 Identify the key words in the question on the right.

2 Do a spider diagram or make notes on some ideas that you could use to answer the question.

Write a speech to give to your year group, informing them about what the school offers out of lesson time. You might wish to mention:
- sports teams
- clubs and societies
- trips.

Structure and paragraphs

Key points

- You will be awarded marks for how well you **structure** your writing.

- That means writing an effective **introduction**, developing your ideas in the **main section**, then ending with a powerful **conclusion**.

- It also means **organising and linking your paragraphs**.

Top Tip!

The time you spend planning your answer is very important. Put your ideas in a logical order, then write a paragraph or two on each main idea.

Pages 50–51

The introduction

- Your first paragraph should **grab the reader's attention**.

- There are **many effective ways** you could do this, e.g. a description, a conversation, a moment of high drama, an anecdote (a story about someone or something).

If your task was 'Describe the person you most admire in the world', you could begin like this:

Opening sentence is relevant – gives an immediate sense of someone you admire.

> Even our mayor admires my Uncle Frank, and gave a dinner in his honour last year. He said: 'What Frank has done is show just how much a person can achieve when they set their mind to it. He has overcome a lot of disadvantages. He's also worked tirelessly for others, even though most people in his position might expect others to look after them. Everyone in this town agrees that he is a great man.'

Quotation makes Frank seem real, and brings the writing to life.

The mayor's speech sets out Frank's qualities and his situation. It shows how much Frank is admired by everyone.

The conclusion

- Your final paragraph should **round off** your piece of writing.

- It should leave the reader with a **good impression**.

- If you can, **link the conclusion with the introduction**.

- Here is a possible ending to the piece of writing on Uncle Frank.

> 'I'm not great, like that mayor said,' Uncle Frank once told me laughing. 'It was kind of him, but I'm just a stubborn man who does what he thinks is right. I've always lived like that, and I always will. I won't give in, but that's not special, it's just the way I am.' But he is special, of course, and that is why I admire him so much.

Good Points

- The student sums up Uncle Frank's character in this anecdote.
- The final sentence links directly to the title.
- The ending refers back to the opening paragraph (the mayor's speech).

Organising and linking paragraphs

- Begin each paragraph with a **topic sentence**. This states the main idea of the paragraph.

- The remaining sentences then develop the idea in more detail, e.g.

  The government has its priorities wrong ...   – you then say why, or what the priorities should be

  There are three steps to perfect happiness ...   – which you then name and discuss

  Please attend to these safety requirements ...   – you then list the safety requirements.

- Link your paragraphs with **connectives** – words or phrases that show the reader you are **linking ideas**. For example:

  - chronological (time sequence), e.g. *At first, Then, Later*
  - logical order, e.g. *Therefore, Consequently, As a result*
  - contrast, e.g. *On the other hand, In contrast*
  - a simple ordering of ideas, e.g. *Firstly, Secondly, Finally*
  - a development of ideas, e.g. *Because of this, What is more, In addition*

Top Tip!

You will gain marks if you vary the length of your paragraphs for effect. A short paragraph, for example, will stand out from the rest.

Look at how this student organises and links her paragraphs in a piece about an eventful holiday:

Grade C

Topic sentence introduces feelings about holidays.

chronological link word

topic sentence

Connective links to previous paragraph.

My holidays used to be boring. I spent my mornings pretending to do the jobs my mother left me before she went to work, and each afternoon I just watched the TV. In the evenings, I just looked out of the window, wishing that something would happen. It even seemed crazy to me at the time, but I wished school would start again so that I could be back with friends. I was even glad that I had a goldfish to talk to. I looked forward to taking my tortoise for walks round the garden.

Then I met Garth, and my life was totally changed. He smiled over the hedge and that was that - he was my new neighbour and he was perfect.

Suddenly, life was better. It was no longer a matter of being bored, it was all about trying to find enough time to get ready and to be with Garth. It was about looking my best and looking out for Garth ...

Long opening paragraph with lists of boring activities – shows the mood of the writer.

Short paragraph for effect: contrasts to what went before and suggests life and change.

Short topic sentence introduces more lively ideas.

Another list, but this time it contrasts with first paragraph: items are shorter, suggesting more life and action.

Task

Find an article at least three paragraphs long in a magazine. Identify the topic sentences and the link words and phrases. Notice how they help you follow the stages of the article. (Noticing how other people write can help you to improve your own writing.)

Sentences

Key points

- Use a **range of sentence length**: short, medium and long.

- Use a **range of sentence types**: statements, questions, commands and exclamations.

- Include **subordinate clauses**, e.g. 'so that ...', 'until ...'

- Make sure the **style** and **tone** of your sentences suit the **purpose** and **audience** of the task.

Short sentences

- Short sentences can produce a **feeling of simplicity**, but that does not mean they cannot be powerful. For example, this moving incident from Ernest Hemingway's *A Farewell to Arms* is mostly made up of short sentences:

> 'Mrs Henry has had a haemorrhage... The doctor is with her.'
>
> 'Is it dangerous?'
>
> 'It is very dangerous.' The nurse went into the room and shut the door. I sat outside in the hall. Everything was gone inside of me. I did not think. I could not think. I knew she was going to die...'

- Short sentences can rush, one after the other, to provide **excitement**:

  He began to run. The man followed. His heart was racing.
  The man was catching him. He had no choice. He dived into the icy water.

- A short sentence after a series of longer sentences can make a **quick but powerful point**:

  The situation right across the country is one that leads many to despair. Hospitals struggling with under-funding and short of both staff and resources are trying to keep our aging population on its feet whilst billions are being wasted on defence contracts and over-spending. It makes me angry.

- A **single word sentence** can create a particular effect, but don't use this technique too much.

  We waited for more information from the governors. Nothing. What a waste of time!

Longer sentences

You can **join two short sentences** together by using 'and', 'so' or 'but':

The Prime Minister has not told the truth.   The Prime Minister has not told the truth **and** he must resign.

He must resign.   The Prime Minister has told the truth **but** he must resign.

- **Longer sentences** often include a subordinate clause, which would not make sense on its own:

  Because the Prime Minister has not told the truth, he must resign.

  The Prime Minister must resign, if he has any sense of honour.

  Although the Prime Minister has resigned, nothing has really changed.

  The Prime Minister has resigned, which is a tragedy.

Top Tip!

If you mix different lengths and types of sentence you will gain marks. In particular, including subordinate clauses makes your sentences much more interesting.

Creating effects

- Longer and more complex sentences are useful for **explaining ideas**:

We cannot overlook the effect on the local wildlife and the countryside, which are bound to suffer. On the other hand, we know how poor the local people are and they must have a say in their own future.

- They provide **more detail** in descriptive writing:

I see the old lady every summer, sitting at the bottom of the steps with her wise eyes and wide smile, and she seems unchanged by the years.

Here is an extract from a piece of descriptive writing:

> These two long sentences set the scene and create an impression of time passing slowly.

At dawn, the sky was grey and there was the sound of crows in the woods behind the house. There was no traffic, just the animals in the fields and the lightest of breezes, rattling the window at times. Then the children were about. The boards started to creak. There were loud voices down the hall.

Grade C

> These three short sentences show action – the house is waking up.

Questions, commands and exclamations

- **Rhetorical questions** do not expect an answer. Instead, they are a way of making a powerful statement:

Do you know any school that has all the facilities it really needs?

– This really means: 'There are no schools that have all the facilities they need.'

Is it ever acceptable to value animals more than humans?

– This really means: 'It is never acceptable to value animals more than humans.'

- **Commands** are a way of addressing the reader directly:

Buy this book and your life will change overnight.

- **Exclamations** show emotional reactions and aim to make the reader react the same way:

What a disgrace!

The results were stunning!

Top Tip!

Different effects suit different purposes and audiences. For example, rhetorical questions are useful when writing to argue or persuade.

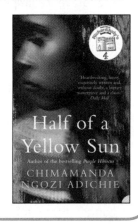

Task

This is an extract from a leaflet about a theme park. Rewrite it so that the sentences are more varied and interesting. You can alter the order and add extra words if you need to.

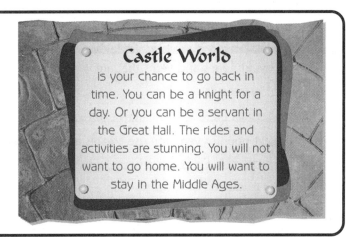

Castle World is your chance to go back in time. You can be a knight for a day. Or you can be a servant in the Great Hall. The rides and activities are stunning. You will not want to go home. You will want to stay in the Middle Ages.

Vocabulary

Key points

- A wide vocabulary helps your writing in many ways, e.g.
  - You can use the **appropriate** word for the **purpose** or **audience**.
  - It means you **avoid repeating** words.
  - It makes your writing **more interesting**.
  - It means you can be **more precise** about the meaning or the effect.
- Use **imagery** to gain higher marks.

Using appropriate words

- Choose words to suit the **purpose** and **audience** of your writing:
  - If you are writing a letter to inform your school or college governors about problems, the language should be **formal**:

  It is with sadness that I have to bring this serious matter to your attention …
  - On the other hand, a letter describing problems to a friend would be **informal**:

  You'll never guess what happened to me. It was some big deal at the time …
  - **Emotive words** (words which persuade the reader to feel something strongly) are useful in persuasive writing, e.g. *broken-hearted, abandoned*.
  - **Technical words** are useful in information writing, e.g. *species, habitat* (for the natural world); *secondary, vocational* (for education).

Avoiding repetition

- In your letter to the governors, for example, instead of repeating 'serious', you might use 'grave' or 'important'.
- The letter to your friend might use a range of different words to describe something bad, e.g. *terrible, awful, tragic, criminal, drastic, mind-numbing*.

Using more interesting words

- Adjectives and adverbs can make your sentences more interesting, e.g.

  The book describes a search, but it is the characters that capture our attention.

  The book describes a <u>mysterious</u> quest, but it is the <u>beautifully-drawn</u> characters that engage our attention.

- Longer, more difficult words are often impressive, e.g. *an <u>atrocious</u> attack, an <u>unacceptable</u> request*.

Using more precise words

- Try to avoid nouns and verbs that are very general, e.g.

  She <u>ran</u> to the <u>shops</u>.

  She <u>jogged all the way</u> to the <u>newsagent's on the corner</u>.

- The exact noun or verb you use creates a **particular effect**, e.g.

  Maria <u>lounged</u> in the <u>conservatory</u>.

  The dog <u>whimpered</u> in the <u>shed</u>.

Top Tip!
Remember to use words and phrases to connect paragraphs and ideas, e.g. 'First', 'Therefore', 'Because of this', 'Yet'.

Page 53

Using imagery

- **Similes** make a comparison using 'like' or 'as':

  Although your father seems <u>as old-fashioned as a sideboard</u>, in this case he is right …

  Your opportunity to work for that company might seem <u>like a ticket to paradise</u> right now, but …

- **Metaphors** state things that are not really true, but the comparison has a strong effect:

  Even though <u>your teachers come from the age of the dinosaurs</u>, they can teach you many things …

  <u>You exploded</u> when I last suggested this, but, <u>at the risk of causing another world war</u>, I must tell you again that …

Top Tip!

When you are checking through your work, don't be afraid to cross words out and replace them with better ones. You will gain marks for using a higher level word, even if it is spelt incorrectly.

'Even though your teachers come from the age of the dinosaurs …'

Notice how this C grade student uses a wide vocabulary, with imagery:

> My life in the hospital kitchen is very different from my existence at school. I slave over sinks of boiling water. There are cooking pots to scrub and I am like a robot: wash the pan, leave it to drain, and move on to the next. Although in school I am with my friends, in my night-time hell I am generally alone. There is just the extreme heat, the sweat from my brow and the clashing of pans for hours on end.

'my existence' avoids repetition of 'my life'

simile

powerful metaphor

precise and powerful verb

linking word

powerful adjective

Task

This is an extract from a student's description of his uncle. Rewrite it to:

- use more interesting and precise words
- avoid repetition (e.g. 'spends a lot of time').

Can you include some imagery?

> At home, Uncle Tom spends a lot of time in his study. That's not because he likes marking school work … it's to get away from Aunt Sylvia. He spends a lot of time in school as well, which is 3 miles down the road.

Punctuation

Key points

- You need to use **basic punctuation**, such as full stops and capital letters.

- To obtain higher marks, you need to use a **range of punctuation**.

- You should **aim to use** commas, apostrophes, question marks and exclamation marks, speech marks, brackets and dashes. If you can use colons and semi-colons, even better.

Commas

- Use commas to:

  1 separate the **items in a list**:

  We have a first class health service, education system and defence force.

  Note that the final item before 'and' (*education system*) does not need a comma after it.

  2 separate **clauses** from the main part of a sentence:

  Although we sometimes doubt politicians, they are working to make our lives better, so we should respect them.

  3 separate a **phrase** that gives extra information about something:

  The Prime Minister, a man of great wisdom, is supported by his ministers.

  4 separate **connectives** that begin sentences:

  Finally, However, Two days later, After all, etc.

Apostrophes

- Apostrophes are used to:

  1 show **possession**:

  – If the 'owner' is singular, the apostrophe goes before the 's', e.g.

  Europe's problems, my aunt's car

  – If the 'owner' is plural, the apostrophe goes after the 's', e.g.

  schools' problems, footballers' wives

  2 show where a letter or letters have been removed (an **omission**), e.g.

  Is not it? ➡ *Isn't it?; You are losing* ➡ *You're losin'*

> **Top Tip!**
> Remember that *its* is used to show ownership (like 'his' or 'hers'), e.g. *She pulled its tail.*
> *It's* (with an apostrophe) stands for 'it is', e.g. *It's raining.*

Question marks and exclamation marks

- Remember to use a **question mark** at the end of every question.

- Don't use too many **exclamation marks**. They should only be used to show humour, or strong or sudden feelings like anger, surprise or delight.

Page 55

In this extract, a doctor explains how he struggles with difficult patients:

Question mark makes it clear how he said the sentence.

You have to be firm with them. On one occasion, an old lady complained so much that I could stand it no longer. 'Problems?' I said. 'You think you have problems? You should try doing my job!'

Comma separates the phrase adding information to the main clause.

Emotion is shown by exclamation mark.

Speech marks

Follow these guidelines:

Put speech marks round the words that are spoken, including any punctuation (here a question mark).

You can even put the speaker in the middle of a spoken sentence, for variety.

'Are you well?' asked my mother.

'He looks strange,' said my father.

I replied, 'I'm as well as could be expected, under the circumstances.'

'In that case,' said my mother, 'we can proceed.'

'But I don't want to go to the dentist,' I said. 'Can't it wait until next week?'

If someone speaks more than one sentence but the speaker is mentioned in between, use a full stop and capital letter, like this.

When the speech is not a question or exclamation, put a comma at the end of it.

If the speaker comes first, add a comma then the speech in speech marks. Begin the speech with a capital letter, and end with a full stop.

Top Tip!

Although you are unlikely to be writing a story in your exam, you might want to include some speech in your response, so you need to know how to punctuate it correctly.

Adding information

- **Brackets** can be used to give extra information, e.g.

His hands lost no speed, his hands looked as fast as Ali's (except when he got hit) and his face was developing a murderous appetite.

The Fight by Norman Mailer

- A **colon** (:) can introduce a list, following a general statement:

  This town can be proud of its heritage: the cathedral, the castle and its famous men and women who fought for what was right.

- A **colon** can also introduce a clause that leads on from or explains the first clause:

  She was terrified: the exam was only three hours away.

- A **semi-colon** links two clauses that are equally important:

  Tammy likes swimming; Katie prefers sailing.

- **Dashes** can be used in the same way.

- Dashes can also **make information stand out**, e.g.

Billionaire Chelsea owner Roman Abramovich has bought himself a new toy – a £72 million yacht.
  The Russian oil tycoon – worth £3.5 billion – stunned onlookers when the 378ft craft put into the South of France last night. *The Sun*

Top Tip!

1 When you write a dash, make sure you include a space before and after it. Otherwise it looks like a hyphen.
2 Don't use dashes too much, as it can look as if you are just adding text thoughtlessly.

Task

1 Add the punctuation to this sentence:
  jakes guitar teacher rang he said hes going to a gig in birmingham

2 Correct the punctuation in this sentence:
  'Its hopeless is'nt it!' she sighed. all the sock's are muddled up

Spelling and accuracy

Key points

- To gain a grade C, you need to spell a wide range of words **accurately**.
- Follow the **spelling rules**, and use **strategies** to master the spelling of difficult words. Most of this should be familiar from Key Stage 3, but it is always good to remind yourself of the rules and strategies.

Spelling rules: plurals

- Add -s to make the plural of a word, e.g. *house* → *houses, pool* → *pools*

Exceptions:

- Words ending in -ss, -sh, -ch, -x: add -es, e.g. *glasses, bushes, matches, foxes*
- Words ending in consonant + y: change -y to -ies, e.g. *lady* → *ladies, try* → *tries*
- Words ending in -f: you usually change -f to -ves, e.g. *loaf* → *loaves, leaf* → *leaves*
- Some words ending in -o: add -es, e.g. *tomatoes, potatoes*
- Some words don't follow these rules, e.g. *children, women, mice, sheep*

Spelling rules: verbs

- Add -ing or -ed to make different parts of the verb, e.g.
  form → *forming* → *formed, watch* → *watching* → *watched*

Exceptions:

- Short verbs ending in vowel + consonant: double the consonant, e.g.
  drop → *dropping* → *dropped, fit* → *fitting* → *fitted*
- Longer verbs ending in vowel + consonant: double the consonant only if the emphasis is on the final syllable, e.g.
  admit → *admitting, prefer* → *preferring,* BUT *benefit* → *benefiting*
- Verbs ending in -e: drop the -e, e.g.
  decide → *deciding* → *decided, state* → *stating* → *stated*
- Many common verbs are irregular in the past tense, e.g.
  fight → *fought, begin* → *began, meet* → *met*

Spelling rules: prefixes and suffixes

- **Prefixes** are letters added at the start of a word to change its meaning:
  - in-, un-, im-, ir-, mis- and dis- often form opposites, e.g. *invisible, unfair, impossible, mistrust*
  - pre- and fore- mean 'in front', 'before', e.g. *prefer, foreground.*
  - Other prefixes include ex- and re- (again), e.g. *export, return.*
- **Suffixes** are letters added at the end of a word to change its meaning:
  - -able, -ible and -uble mean that something is possible, e.g. *legible, soluble.*
  - -ful means 'full of', e.g. *careful, peaceful* (NB not -full).
  - -less means 'without', e.g. *careless, endless*
  - -ation, -ition, -ution form a noun from a verb, e.g.
    create → *creation, pollute* → *pollution*
  - Drop a final -e before a suffix that begins with a vowel, e.g.
    invite + -ation = invitation, forgive + -able = forgivable

Spelling strategies

- The best way to master spelling is to look words up in a **dictionary** while you are writing. (You cannot use a dictionary in the exam.)

- Do **not** use **spell checker** programs. They don't tell you if a word is spelt correctly, only if it exists – and they make you a lazy speller.

- Compile a **list** of words you often misspell. Learn the correct spellings.

- **Learn** these words that are often misspelt.

all right	business	environment	occasionally
argument	coming	favourite	persuade
beautiful	definitely	friend	receive
beginning	develop	immediately	sense
believe	disappear	necessary	separate

Know the difference

- Some common words **sound the same** but are spelt differently. Learn these and look out for others:

  your (belonging to you) and you're (you are)

  their (belonging to them), they're (they are) and there (any other use)

  where (place), were (verb) and we're (we are)

  too (as well or very), two (the number) and to (any other use)

  whose (belonging to someone), who's (who is)

  quiet (calm), quite (a bit)

  accept (take), except (apart from)

  effect (noun), affect (verb)

> **Top Tip!**
> Don't be afraid to make alterations. However, although there are no marks for neatness, you must make sure the end result is legible, or you will lose marks.

Other spelling tips

- Use **mnemonics** (memory joggers), e.g.
  Remember there is *iron* in the *environment*, a *rat* in *separate*, *finite* in *definite* and a *cog* in *recognise*.

- Group words into **families**, where part of the word is the same, e.g.
  success, successful, succeed; *writing, writer, written*

- **Say the word** in your mind as it is spelt, e.g.
  Fe*bru*ary, Wed*nes*day

- **Chunking** – break words into smaller parts, e.g.
  ex-treme-ly, re-le-vant

Checking and correcting

- Spend five minutes at the end **checking** and **improving** your writing. This is important because vocabulary, punctuation and spelling **can all be improved**.

- **Read** through your response very slowly, as if reading aloud, and be prepared to **alter** your work whenever necessary.

Task

Check this writing and correct the spelling mistakes.

> Why we should eat healthy food
> People should except the arguement that eating healthy food is good for us. It makes our weight disapear and has a good sychologicle affect on our state of mind. It doesnt matter if we ocasionaly have a cake or some choclate, but we should definately eat fruit and vegatables every day and losts of fruit; that's the only way to improof ourselfs and our society.

Writing to argue

Key points

- One of the questions in Section B of Paper 1 lets you **write to argue**.

- When you write to argue, you **present and develop a point of view** about something.

- Your answer should refer to the **other point of view**, be **well structured** and use **techniques** to convince the reader.

Presenting a point of view

- Your main task is to present your **point of view**. For example, it could be that students should wear school uniform, or that people should not eat meat.

- Make your point of view **clear from the start** of your answer.

- In your planning, jot down some ideas that **support** your point of view. Then note some **opposing** ideas. Think about how you would answer these points.

- Show that you are **aware of the opposite point of view** by referring to it in your answer.

In this extract, a student is arguing that there should be more money for schools.

> **Top Tip!**
>
> It helps if you believe in the point of view that you are arguing for. However, if you don't have a personal view on the issue, it doesn't matter. Choose one side of the argument and pretend that you are passionate about it!

Writer's own view is clear from the start.

The opposite viewpoint is referred to very briefly, but immediately attacked (note: 'But').

> We all know that more money is needed for schools. The extra books and equipment it can buy help them improve. We can see this because independent schools charge fees and use them to buy all the latest books and technology, and they have a good reputation.
>
> Yes, the government points out that the quality of teaching is the most important thing. But teaching must be better when every student has a book and does not have to share, or has a PC on which to access the internet. So funding is vital for schools.

Grade C

Reason for view is explained, and an example given (independent schools).

Writer's own point of view is stated strongly again.

Good Points

- The student's view is clear from the start.
- There is a brief mention of the other side of the argument.
- The opposite viewpoint is immediately dismissed so that the writer's own point of view can be developed.

Structure

- When you write an argument, you should be as **clear and logical** as possible. Structure is important.

- Make sure the main points are covered in a **logical and sensible order**.

- Begin a **new paragraph** for each **new point**.

- Introduce each main point with a **topic sentence**. The other sentences should develop that point.

Page 53

- Use **connectives** to show the links between points, such as 'however', 'on the other hand'.

- Make an impact on the reader with your **introduction** and **conclusion**.

Introduction

- Your introduction (paragraph 1) should **present the topic** and **state your attitude** to it.

Compare these two introductions, which have been given different grades. The 'How To Improve' box tells you the main points to improve in order to move the Grade D response to a Grade C. The students are writing an article for an employers' magazine, to argue for or against work experience.

> When I was told about work experience I wondered whether I would like it, and it was quite a difficult thing to do but in the end I quite liked it. Some people say work experience is a waste of time, and I know what they mean because I felt that too. Though I suppose it helps students get to know what real life is like.

Grade D

How To Improve

- The student presents the topic of work experience, but it isn't clear what his or her point of view is. Is the argument for or against work experience?
- The student moves from work experience being difficult, to it being enjoyable, to it being useful – this is confusing for the reader.

Point of view is stated at start.

Opposite point of view is referred to, then dismissed.

> In my opinion, work experience is a good thing. Some people argue that it is a waste of time, but I am going to show that it helps students get to know what real life is like. There are many things in its favour ...

Grade C

Good Points

- The student's point of view is clear from the start.
- There is some reference to another point of view.
- The student shows how s/he is going to develop the argument (by discussing the things in favour of work experience).
- The style is formal, which suits the purpose and audience.

TYPES OF WRITING

Development

- The main part of your answer should **develop your main points** logically. You can do this by:
  - giving **reasons** for your opinion
  - going into your points in more **detail**
  - giving one or more **examples**
  - providing some **evidence** for your views, e.g. facts and figures, personal experience, quotations from other people.

Look at this plan, by a student who did his work experience in a garage.

> **Top Tip!**
> As part of the planning, jot down the main points of your arguments. Put them in a sensible order, then follow this plan to give a good structure to the main part of your answer.
> *Pages 50–51*

PLAN

Introduction

Para 2: what I learnt about working in a team
    responsibilities/being supported

Para 3: how I enjoyed the tasks
    taking apart engines/breakdown outings

Para 4: what I learnt that I would not have learnt at school
    dealing with real problems/longer hours

Para 5: what happened to my friends
    bad bosses/boring work/unfriendly workmates

Para 6: why it is a good experience
    school is too protected/we will have to work

Conclusion:
    why it was so useful

main point

idea for developing the main point

> **Good Points** ✓
> - The argument is developed logically:
>   - what he got out of it
>   - others' problems
>   - why it is still valuable.
> - Different viewpoints are included.
> - Each main point is given a new paragraph.
> - There is an introduction and conclusion.

Conclusion

- The **conclusion** should sum up your opinion.
- Try to write an ending which will **stick in the memory**. Don't just tail off ...

> **Top Tip!**
> The conclusion is the last thing the examiner will read before giving you a mark, so make it as clear and lively as possible.

So, when I looked back on the two weeks, I realised that the problems didn't mean I hadn't learnt a lot and enjoyed myself. It was great to be covered in oil and I even feel that I am now better prepared for a working life. I would recommend work experience to anyone!

Grade C

> **Good Points** ✓
> - The student makes it clear that he is summing up ('So, when I looked back ...').
> - The main point of view is stated again.
> - It is a personal response, not a general statement.
> - The conclusion is positive and enthusiastic.

Using a range of techniques

- Use a variety of techniques to present your argument effectively:
  - **anecdotes**: telling a story about someone/something that backs up your point
  - **quotations**: quoting what experts say
  - **rhetorical questions**: questions that are really a strong way of stating your view
  - **direct address**: addressing the reader directly to make them think about the point you are making
  - **lists**: building up a list of facts or evidence to make your point strongly
  - **varying the length** of your sentences.

This extract from a letter to the local council includes many of these techniques. It argues that more needs to be done for local residents.

rhetorical question

Topic sentence introduces opposite point of view.

Words of an 'expert' are quoted, then argued against.

list of problems

Grade C

> Dear Sir,
>
> Does our city have to have graffiti and litter and loads of junk in the streets? You collect our taxes and say you are concerned about our problems, but nothing ever seems to improve. I am tired of living in slum conditions on my housing estate, and I know that you can do something about it. You need a positive drive to improve our quality of life.
>
> We often receive your leaflets, telling us how our neighbourhoods are safer and cleaner and how new action schemes are making our lives better. But we do not believe it. When the mayor writes:
>
> 'We can celebrate, because studies show all the improvements in our lives'
>
> we are simply amazed. He seems to have no idea of what it is really like.
>
> If you ever bothered to visit us you would see the truth for yourself. Our bins are always overflowing. There are abandoned cars, which teenagers love torching. The walls of buildings are covered in graffiti ...

direct address

strong statement of the point of view

Connective shows the reader that the view is going to be criticised.

effective short sentence to end paragraph

Good Points

- The writer has made his or her point of view clear, and referred to another viewpoint.
- The letter has a clear and logical structure.
- It begins with a powerful introduction which states the point of view.
- It uses techniques such as rhetorical question, quotation and list.
- The reader is guided through the text by topic sentences and connectives.

Task

Write an article for a local newspaper, arguing that your town, village or city needs improvement.

- Give it a clear and logical structure.
- State your point of view, but refer to a different viewpoint as well.
- Include some techniques to make your readers agree with your argument.

Writing to persuade

Key points

- One of the questions in Section B of Paper 1 lets you **write to persuade**.

- When you write to persuade, you try to get the reader to **do something or believe something**.

- Your answer should be **well structured** and use **techniques** to convince the reader.

- It should have a **tone** that suits the **purpose** and the **audience** of the task.

Structuring ideas

- As part of the **planning**, jot down your main ideas.

- Put them in a **sensible order** so that one idea **flows logically** from another.

- Then develop your main points by adding **further ideas**.

- Follow your plan to give a good structure to your answer.

Look at this plan for a letter to persuade an elderly relative to protect herself against dangers in the home.

Pages 50–51

> **Top Tip!**
>
> There are different ways of persuading people. You might want to persuade readers by presenting a logical argument. In that way, persuasion can be like writing to argue.
>
> When you persuade, however, you don't have to include more than one point of view.
>
> For example, you might be writing a letter to persuade an elderly relative to protect herself against dangers in the home (as in the plan below). All you need to do is stress the need for more protection. You don't have to wonder if she may already be well protected.

main point

idea for developing the main point

PLAN

Intro: the need to be secure

    she is an important part of the family

Para 2: action needed to protect her against burglars

    needs modern locks, an alarm, etc.

Para 3: other problems

    old gas cooker; bad wiring

Para 4: the benefits which will come from greater protection

    she can be more relaxed; cheaper home insurance

Conclusion:

    how everyone in the family will feel better knowing she is safe

her need

↓

problems

↓

benefits from taking action

> **Good Points**
>
> - The plan sets out ideas in a sensible order. It lists the current problems and then moves on to the benefits which would come from taking action.
> - The main points are given (underlined), then developed by giving detail and examples.
> - The introduction stresses the dangers but the conclusion stresses the benefits, so the persuasion has a clear direction.

Emotive language

- **Emotive language** is language which makes the reader feel something. It is a very effective technique when writing to persuade.

This is part of Nelson Mandela's speech when he was sworn in as the first black president of South Africa. Note the emotive language (in purple). Think about what the president wants to make the audience feel.

> We dedicate this day to the heroes and heroines in this country and the rest of the world who sacrificed in many ways and surrendered their lives so that we could be free. Their dreams have become reality. Freedom is their reward.

Compare these two opening paragraphs to persuade Grandma to make herself more secure. They have been awarded different grades:

> You are not safe in your home! I'm really worried that someone could break in or that you could be harmed by a fire! Your gas fires and cooker have not been checked recently! Why not!! Just follow my suggestions, and you'll be alright.

Grade D

How To Improve

- The student addresses Grandma, but the language is general. It needs some emotive language to make the reader feel something. All the feeling at the moment is coming from the exclamation marks.
- The exclamation marks produce a very sharp tone which might frighten Grandma. More reassuring language is needed in places.
- The student needs to begin the letter with 'Dear Grandma'.

Makes reader think how nice this would be.

Makes reader feel lonely and afraid.

Makes reader imagine the fire engine, and so the fire.

> Dear Grandma,
> I have been thinking about the fact that you are not as safe and cosy in your home as you might be. I am concerned about the dark and lonely nights. I worry about fire whenever I hear a fire engine's sirens. Please listen to the suggestions I have to make.

Grade C

Good Points

- Emotive language and precise details make the reader picture things happening and feel afraid.
- The student uses a caring tone, which is suitable for the audience (Grandma).
- The writing includes persuasion from the start.

67

TYPES OF WRITING

Examples and anecdotes

- Develop the points you are making by **giving examples**.

- **Include an anecdote**. Anecdotes are like very short stories which prove your point. Writing about what has actually happened can be very convincing.

The Grade C student is now writing about Grandma's security measures:

An example develops the main point made in the first sentence.

Anecdote gives a 'real' example of something that has happened.

> You need to have more security around you to be safe. For example, when we moved into our new house, Dad fitted new door locks and a chain and we felt better immediately. At the moment you aren't protected against thieves, so anyone could break in. Last year when my friend's parents woke up to find a burglar in their bedroom, it terrified them. I wouldn't want you to go through that.

Good Points

- The general statement ('You need to have more security') is followed by precise detail (the example).
- The anecdote develops and illustrates the point being made.

Rhetoric

- **Rhetoric** is 'language used for effect'. Using rhetoric when writing to persuade will gain you extra marks.

- Some good **rhetorical techniques** are:

    - **imagery** (similes and metaphors): to paint a picture in the reader's mind, e.g.

    you are <u>as valuable to us as the crown jewels</u>

    - **exaggeration**: overstating a view to impress the audience, e.g.

    <u>every day</u> you are in danger …

    - **contrast**: putting two opposites together to create an effect, e.g.

    we want you to be <u>safe</u>, but we fear constant <u>danger</u>

    - **using 'I', 'we', 'you'**, etc: to make the writing more personal, and address the reader, e.g.

    <u>You</u> have to be safe, so that <u>we</u> can be happy.

    - **repetition**: repeating the same word or phrase, e.g.

    <u>we want you safe</u> from burglars, and <u>we want you safe</u> from all other dangers

    - **rhetorical questions**: to challenge the reader, e.g.

    Is there any reason why you shouldn't make these improvements straight away?

    - **humour**: to win the reader over to your view, e.g.

    Don't forget, you have to be perfectly safe so you can cook me my tea whenever I'm passing!

Using a range of techniques

This student has tried to use all the techniques covered in this section.

Write an article for a national newspaper persuading more people to vote.

Rhetorical question creates a powerful opening and demands the reader's attention.

An example is given.

Examples (TV and darts) are given to illustrate the point.

emotive language

emotive language

Grade C

Clear point of view is hammered home by short sentence at end of paragraph.

Emotive language makes you feel for the victims and the simile adds a powerful detail.

Anecdote highlights main point of article.

direct address ('you')

Why everyone should vote

How many times have you heard someone at the bus stop complaining about taxes or transport? These people usually say they don't vote anyway, because it does no good. But if they don't vote, they have no right to complain. It is as simple as that.

Think about people around the world, they would give almost anything to be allowed to vote for what they believe in. They are tortured when they speak out and often die like animals because they can't vote.

In contrast, so many people nowadays choose to ignore the ballot box, saying that it is pointless. They say their vote is meaningless and a waste of time. As if watching television or playing darts in the pub isn't a waste of time. People have given their lives so that we might have the vote, but that means nothing to many people.

A programme on TV looked at government in Africa. There was a man who queued for ten hours to vote and it was the first time he had been able to. It makes you think how different it is in our society.

So when the next election comes around, you should find the time to vote because it represents your right to choose. You should vote if you care about our country.

Good Points

- The text is persuasive throughout.
- A range of techniques is used effectively.
- There is a powerful opening and conclusion.
- Sentences and vocabulary are varied.

Task

Write the script of a talk to be given on radio. Its aim is to persuade the listeners to become more involved in helping charities.

Structure your talk effectively, and include:
- emotive language
- at least one example or anecdote
- rhetoric.

Writing to advise

Key points

- One of the questions in Section B of Paper 1 lets you **write to advise**.

- When you write to advise, you are helping someone **to do something** or **to behave in a particular way**.

- You should **organise**, **plan** and **present your ideas**.

- You should use the **right tone**, offer **solutions** to the problems and use **examples**.

Organising your ideas

- There are **two methods** you can use when organising your ideas. You could:

  1 First set out a problem in a lot of detail, e.g. how problems with parents can become very serious, **then** offer advice , e.g. how to avoid these problems.

  OR

  2 Set out the advice **as you go**. For each problem, offer some advice, e.g.

The first thing you mention in your letter is …	*I think that you need to tackle this in three different ways …*
You then go on to explain that …	*In this particular case, you might consider …*
Then, there is your concern about …	*If I were you, I would …*

- Make sure you choose **one** of these methods and stick to it. Don't mix the two together.

Planning

- If your advice is logical, it will be convincing. To make your advice logical you need to:

  1 show **what the problem involves**

  2 explain **what can be done about it**.

- Make sure that you cover both these things in your **planning**. A good plan will include ideas of **problems**, and ideas of possible **solutions**.

- This Grade C student was asked to write a section of the school brochure, offering advice to new students about settling in at school. This was her plan. Note the problems, followed by the ideas about solutions.

PLAN

Intro: outline of all the problems

      complicated timetable, big school, confusing layout, moving each lesson, masses of students and teachers

Para 2: how to understand the timetable

      why it's necessary, use student planner

Para 3: how to find your way around

      map in planner and on corridors, asking for help

Para 4: how to cope with students

      avoid bullies, get help from form tutor

Para 5: how to cope with teachers

      obey the rules, show respect

Conclusion:

Good Points

- The plan is logical. Problems are briefly outlined in the introduction, then each one is given its own paragraph.
- Advice is offered at each stage ('how to …').

Presenting your ideas

- You may be asked to present your advice in a **particular form**, e.g. a letter, leaflet, advice sheet, speech, magazine article.

- Think about how your **presentation suits the form**. For example, an advice sheet will include **subheadings** to break up the text.

- You could also include **numbers**, **flowcharts** or **bullet points**.

Top Tip!

Don't waste time adding graphics, logos or other illustrations to your answer. You will only earn marks for the *words* you use, and the way you structure your response.

For example:

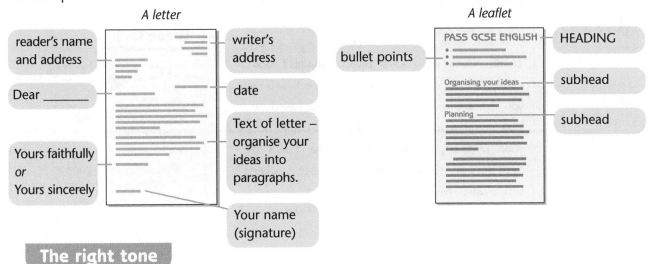

A letter

reader's name and address

writer's address

Dear _____

date

Yours faithfully
or
Yours sincerely

Text of letter – organise your ideas into paragraphs.

Your name (signature)

A leaflet

bullet points

PASS GCSE ENGLISH — HEADING

Organising your ideas — subhead

Planning — subhead

The right tone

- As with all your writing, make sure the tone suits the **purpose** and **audience**. You need to **address the reader** from the outset, and keep the reader in mind the whole time.

- Use different words and phrases to **vary your tone**:

  - **Commands** tell the reader directly what to do. (Be careful not to use too many though, or you might sound a bit harsh.)

  Take the first chance you get …

  Ask the teacher …

  Don't forget your planner …

  - **'Must'** and **'should'** also make it sound really important that the reader does what you are saying:

  You must learn from others …

  You should not be late …

  - **Softer words** to use are 'can', 'may', 'might' or 'could':

  You could ask a teacher …

  You might like to put your planner …

  - **'If … (then) …'** sets out the result of taking advice (you don't have to include the word 'then'):

  If you adopt a positive attitude, (then) …

- This extract from a Grade C response includes some of these different ways of giving advice.

Don't worry when you come to our school. You need to get to grips with a whole new situation, including the crowds, the size of the school and all the new people. Take a deep breath but try not to panic. If you keep your cool, you will soon get used to it all.

Good Points

- The commands offer clear advice.
- The other approaches have a softer tone. They will make the newcomer more confident.
- The mix of the two approaches makes the writing varied.

Offering solutions

- As part of your advice, you need to **offer solutions** to the problems.

The plan on pages 70–71 is for an answer that sets out the advice as it goes along. Each section, therefore, needs:

- – a **description** of the problem
- – suggested **solutions**, explaining why they will be effective.

This extract deals with the problem of understanding the school timetable:

description of the problem

first solution offered, plus explanation (because ...)

second solution offered, plus explanation (so ...)

> You will have to cope with strange lesson times, which vary each day. I suggest you always wear a watch, because that will help you to avoid becoming totally confused. You could also look at the timetable in your planner, which gives you the times of each lesson, so you will know exactly where you ought to be and when.

Grade C

Good Points

- The paragraph is set out very clearly: problem, solution 1 + explanation, solution 2 + explanation.
- What needs to be done is straightforward and logical: use a watch and the planner.
- The advice is given in a soft tone ('I suggest you ...', 'you could also ...'), to give the reader confidence.

Using examples

- You can make your advice more convincing by **using examples**:

  Think about what happened when ...

  It is worth remembering ...

Examples link your advice to what has happened in the past. This reassures the reader. The advice seems easier to trust.

This is how you could **conclude**:

example which looks back to previous successes

makes advice sound easy to follow

> If you accept the advice offered in this booklet you should be fine. Other students who have followed this advice have settled down within a week or so. One said last year: 'I've only been here two weeks, and it feels like home already.' All you need to do is what others have done before you.
>
> So make every effort to blend in, work hard and your future should be rosy.

Grade C

quotation to support the point being made

Top Tip!

Think about adding some quotations from other people to back up the points you are making. They make your answer more varied, too.

enthusiastic final sentence

Using a range of techniques

Try to use all the techniques dealt with in this section, as in the answer below.

> Write an article for a travel magazine, to advise travellers on how to cope with foreign languages.

Appropriate tone for this sort of magazine article: it interests and entertains.

Why you will benefit.

First definite advice: 'if you're sensible' softens the tone.

sound piece of advice

Persuasive conclusion: clever use of language makes the advice more acceptable.

> Grade C

The British speak English and expect the rest of the world to do the same. If some foreigner does not speak English, then we shout at him, and he will get the idea!

But most of the British who go abroad now realise that they have to speak a bit of the 'lingo' to get the most out of their time. They can then get on better with the locals and feel as if they have really been somewhere foreign. They can feel less like people on holiday and more like people travelling.

It is hard to do this straight off, so if you're sensible you need to do some work at home. Language guides are a great start. It is amazing how good you feel if you can ask for bread or order a drink in another language. My brother, who is only seven, loved going to the bakery when we were in France and ordering bread for breakfast. He always came back smiling.

You could learn from the signs around you, from menus and just from what you hear in the street. You could ask people what they call knives and forks etc. They will even teach you whole sentences once you show an interest – and you can pick it up really quickly.

It is simply a matter of making the effort and then enjoying the results. Travel broadens the mind, they say – it can also broaden your language skills!

Ideas organised logically. The old situation is described in paragraph 1, the new approach in paragraph 2.

Positive comment: benefits are pointed out.

Example proves the point.

Appropriate examples given.

Can you understand English??!!!

> **Good Points**
> - The response presents situations, offers solutions and suggests likely outcomes.
> - The tone is light but presents some serious points.
> - The examples give the advice more credibility.
> - The introduction and conclusion are memorable.
> - The answer develops logically.
> - Language is used effectively.

Task

Your school has been given a grant of £100,000 from the government. On behalf of your year group, write a letter to your headteacher to offer advice on how the school should spend it.

Writing to inform

Key points

- One of the questions in Section B of Paper 2 lets you **write to inform**.

- The information should be **clear**, **detailed** and **relevant**.

- **Organise your ideas** well.

- Include **facts** and **opinions**.

- Add **personal feelings and experiences** to gain extra marks.

Top Tip!

It is much better to write in depth about a few points than to try to cover everything in a very general way. Try to focus on the most important points and include as much detail as possible.

Choosing the information

- Information texts aim to tell someone about something.

- Begin by **planning**. Jot down your ideas in brief, as in this **spider diagram**.

> Write a letter to a pen friend who is about to visit from abroad, to tell them about the area in which you live.

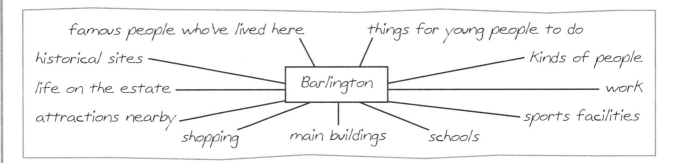

famous people who've lived here · things for young people to do · historical sites · Kinds of people · life on the estate · *Barlington* · work · attractions nearby · sports facilities · shopping · main buildings · schools

- Now decide which are the **most important** points, and focus on those.

Organising your ideas

- Organise your points so that similar ideas are covered at the same time.

- Look at the detailed plan below. Each main topic is given a new paragraph. A few significant points of information are covered in each topic.

Introduction gives summary.	PLAN _Intro: general details_ looking forward to the visit, much to find out about, many things to see
Begins close to home.	_Para 2: what is nearby_ neighbours, the estate – shops and houses
Moves out to wider town.	_Para 3: the town_ employment, schools, facilities
Then mentions other interesting features.	_Para 4: what's worth seeing_ historical sites, buildings, attractions
	Para 5: other points of interest youth culture, recent improvements
Ends with summary.	_Conclusion: summary of Barlington_ some fun, some interest

Good Points

- Most of the ideas in the spider diagram are included in this detailed plan.
- They are organised into particular topics, one per paragraph.
- There is a logical development: introduction – nearby – town itself – famous features – other points of interest – summary.

Facts and opinions

- Make sure you include a mixture of facts and opinions.
  - The **facts** provide the basic detail.
  - The **opinions** tell the reader what you think about the information. Opinions give it a more personal focus.

This student has provided a mixture of facts and opinions in her **introduction**.

> Dear Gabbi,
>
> We are really looking forward to your visit. I thought I would tell you all about where we live, so there will be no surprises when you arrive. There are many good things here. We are surrounded by history, which can be quite fascinating. Also, there are some unusual things. Some of the families around us seem a bit odd, but they aren't dangerous!

Pages 8–9

Top Tip!

Remember:
Facts are things that we know are true, e.g. information about when a building was built.
Opinions are what the writer believes or feels about the facts, e.g. whether s/he likes the building.

Good Points

- Student includes some **facts** – what she is going to do; the place is full of history.
- The **opinions** make it more personal – 'good things', 'fascinating', 'unusual', 'odd'.

Making the information clear

- When you write to inform, you must make the **information clear**. Assume that the reader knows nothing about what you are describing.

- The **more detail** you can give, the clearer your information will be.

- **Link the paragraphs** to show how all the information connects together.

The letter to Gabbi needs to be absolutely clear, because she probably has no knowledge of the local area.

Links with previous paragraph.

Details make information clear and interesting.

Further detail given.

> We do, though, have some attractions which you will find interesting. My parents plan to take us to the castle, which is in all the history books. It was the site of a famous battle during the Wars of the Roses and I think in the Civil War too. From the top, you get great views of the countryside around. You can almost imagine the soldiers fighting and dying as you watch from the walls. The museum there shows many of the weapons and tells you more about how the battles were organised ...

Grade C

personal opinion

Personal response – she paints a picture of her watching from the castle.

Good Points

- The detail and personal response bring the facts about the castle to life.
- The paragraph has been linked to the one before.

TYPES OF WRITING

Personal response

- Try to provide a **personal response**. That means including your **feelings** about things. Referring to your own experience is much more powerful than just providing a list of details.

- It is especially important to give your personal response in your **conclusion**. When you sum up for the reader you should give your own view about the information.

This is how one student ended the letter to her friend:

> You will be able to experience the things I have told you about, and give us your opinions on them. Personally, I am certain you will enjoy the sports facilities best – but we will see whether I am right.
> Best wishes ...

Grade D

This makes a more effective ending:

Shows that you are summing up.

Note variety of sentence types, and use of adjectives to add colour and detail.

> You should now have a good picture of what it is like here and we hope you will have a wonderful time while you are with us. You will be given a really warm welcome. I can promise you many things to do: guided tours of our historical buildings, fun afternoons at the sports centre, and great evenings with my crazy friends.
>
> To complete your 'English' holiday you will be treated to a huge helping of fish and chips at the local chippy, which will give you something to remember when you get home!

Grade C

Final example of what the area has to offer, and personal opinion on the effect it will have.

Good Points ✓

- The response gives a personal view but is still informative.
- The writer's opinion suggests it will all be enjoyable.
- The sentences and the use of language are varied.
- The letter comes to an effective ending, by imagining the last day and the guest returning home.

Top Tip!

Remember to make your information writing lively and interesting:

- Use different lengths and types of sentence.

Pages 54–55 →

- Use colourful or powerful words instead of plain, general words.

Pages 56–57 →

Using a range of techniques

Try to use all the techniques dealt with in this section, as in the answer below.

Write an article for a national newspaper, to inform the readers about the problems faced by modern teenagers.

Grade C

1st paragraph links with title and briefly covers all the topics. Shows good planning.

2nd paragraph covers topic of being treated like children. Detailed examples are given of life at home.

3rd paragraph covers topic of life outside the home. This is made clear in the link 'outside the home'.

4th paragraph covers topic of school. Note link words 'at school' and varied sentence structure.

5th paragraph sums up problems and gives contrast with older people.

It has never been easy to be a teenager, and it is very difficult today. The world expects us to be grown up but we aren't treated like adults. We live in a dangerous society, for example where drugs are readily available. At school we have exam after exam and we have to cope with growing up as well, so it's hardly any wonder that we struggle at times.

One of the biggest problems is that adults want us to be mature but they still treat us like children. We help around the house, but we're told to come back by a certain time at night. We are expected to get a part-time job to earn money, but we don't have a say about where we go for the family holiday.

Outside the home, there are dangers everywhere. Older people had alcohol and cigarettes, that's true, but it was easy by comparison. We go to a club, then are faced with drug dealers and pressure from friends and our own need to fit in with the crowd. Then there are all the designer clothes that tempt us too. Being a teenager has never been harder.

At school we have so many exams, it is difficult to keep track: SATs, GCSEs, coursework, mocks .... We get homework every night. The teachers work us harder and harder because they have to improve results or their own careers will suffer.

And teenagers are suffering from hormones, relationship problems, and changes in their bodies. I suppose our parents and grandparents suffered the same, but they didn't have all the other modern pressures we have. They are lucky they were born at another time.

Good Points

- The writer presents detailed information in an organised way.
- The facts are supported and illustrated by opinions.
- The language and style suit the purpose and audience of the task.

Task

Write informatively about a pastime you enjoy.

Note: In a task of this kind, you should assume your audience is the examiner.

Writing to explain

Key points

- One of the questions in Section B of Paper 2 lets you **write to explain**.
- Explaining is **different from just giving information**.
- Writing to explain requires:
    - good **structure** and **planning**
    - content which sets out **how or why** something occurs, rather than just what happens
    - clear but interesting **language**.

> **Top Tip!**
>
> Many students lose marks because they don't *explain* the subject they are writing about. Examiners will be looking for explanation. Don't just write information.

Structure and planning

- Explaining something means helping someone understand. Your structure has to be clear. This means paying special attention to your planning.

Think about this title:

> Most people have memories of a particular holiday or trip.
> Choose one that you have experienced, and explain why it was so memorable.

> **Top Tip!**
>
> This question does *not* ask you to:
> - write about trips in general
> - describe what happened on one special trip
> - write a lot of information about the place you visited.
>
> It *does* ask you to:
> - decide what made one trip special and say why
> - select memorable features of the trip and explain why they are memorable.

Your plan might look like this:

> PLAN
> <u>Intro:</u> where we went, why memorable
>   Turkey, highs and lows
> <u>Para 2: first part fun</u>
>   beaches, food, friends: show why
> <u>Para 3: dad's nightmare</u>
>   drunken evening, people complaining,
>   explain what happened
> <u>Para 4: mum bitten by cat</u>
>   rabies fears, hospital, how it went from
>   bad to worse
> <u>Para 5: leaving</u>
>   people friendly: explain it still didn't
>   take away the horror
> <u>Conclusion: never going back!</u>
>   problems bigger than pleasures

> **Top Tip!**
>
> Choose only a few points to write about. It is better to explain a few points in detail, rather than trying to include too much material.

> **Good Points**
>
> - The plan is organised clearly. The introduction shows two sides to the holiday. More detail is given in the following paragraphs.
> - There is a focus on explanation throughout: 'why', 'explain', and 'how' are all important words in this plan.

OR:

You could plan by linking some text bubbles like this. (The main point is inside the bubble. The lines branching off each bubble give examples or go into more detail. They develop the main point.)

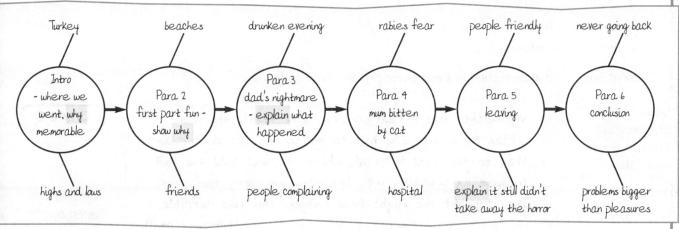

Introduction

• It is a good idea to **explain from the beginning** of your answer. This shows the examiner that you are not just writing information or description. It will also help to keep you focused on the task.

Look at how these students approach the task differently:

> About six years ago, I went on holiday with my family to Turkey. We wanted to go to Turkey for years, and finally we were there. We stayed in a place called Datca, it was on the coast and very hot. And there were not many British people there. We had some good times and some bad times and I am going to tell you about the bad times.

Grade D

How To Improve

• There is a clear first sentence, setting the scene, but the student does not explain why it was a memorable holiday.
• It is treated more like an information text ('I am going to tell you').

> About six years ago, I went on holiday with my family to Turkey. We stayed in a place called Datca, and there were not many British people there. I am sure we could have had a good time and then it would have been 'just another holiday'. However, there were also some seriously bad moments which made the holiday especially memorable.

Grade C

Good Points

• It gives clear background information.
• Then it implies it was special – not 'just another holiday'.
• It refers to the key word in the question – 'memorable'.
• Begins to explain and focuses on the title.

Top Tip!

Even if you are asked to write about your own experiences, you don't have to tell a true story. You can either make it up altogether, or base the story on something that happened. Whichever you do, you need to make it believable.

TYPES OF WRITING

'How' and 'why'

- When you write to explain, you are **giving reasons**, saying **why** or **how** something happens (or happened).

- A good way of doing this is to:
  - describe a **situation**
  - say **why** or **how** it came about
  - describe the **effect** it had.

Look at how the middle section of this answer explains how and why:

Describes the situation and explains how it came about.

Explains the effect on the family.

> My mother had a real problem. One night, she was bitten by a cat. She had to go to see the doctor and then to the local hospital, where she was told she had to have an injection into her stomach every two days. They thought she might have rabies. This was terrible, and made our holiday a nightmare. My mother was really frightened, and cried quite often. The injections really hurt her, and it is not something we will ever forget.

Grade C

Links to the question, explaining why it has made such an impression.

Using the right language

- The explanation must be **clear**, so that the reader understands it perfectly.

- Some **phrases** are useful to make your explanations clear:

1 Phrases to explain **the reasons and causes of something**:

Because   So   Therefore

As a result of this

This meant that

This is because

The reason for this

As a consequence

2 Phrases to show when something is **uncertain**:

It could be

It may be that

It might be that

Perhaps

Top Tip!

- In your conclusion, try to sum up the key points of the explanation. In this case, it would be what made the trip memorable.
- It is also your chance to refer back to the question. This shows you have been focusing on the question throughout, which always impresses the examiner.

Some of these phrases have been used in this conclusion:

'might be' suggests a possible explanation.

Explains again why the trip was so memorable.

Still explaining how they were affected.

> It might be that what happened to my mother has had a real effect on what I think about Turkey. It is a beautiful country, and has friendly people, but my mother had a terrible time, my father was really cut up, and the rest of us just felt helpless. This meant that things we wanted to enjoy, like the beach, were forgotten, and instead we remember the hospital visits. Also, things we laughed about at the time, such as my dad's experience when he got drunk, we couldn't laugh about afterwards. My mother was in pain, so we remember that and nothing else, really.

Grade C

Phrase introduces an explanation.

Good Points

- The holiday is summarised in the conclusion.
- The effects of the bad time are explained: we know why it was so memorable and how they reacted.

Using all the techniques

Try to use all the techniques dealt with in this section, as in the answer below.

> Explain what you most dislike about television.

Grade C

Begins with a positive, but then goes on to show the other side.

I am sure that television is not all bad. However, what is on TV in my house is awful. In fact it kills off brain cells. I am sick of soaps and reality television above all.

Daytime television isn't even worth talking about, it is beneath contempt, but even in the evening the programmes are just boring. The soaps drip on and on, as interesting as watching golf. Everyone in the programme spends every night in the pub having disasters; and we sit on our settees eating our tea and lapping up the rubbish, because there seems to be no alternative.

Unfortunately, reality shows make everything worse. Because they haven't got anything better to do, people sit and watch non-celebrities swearing at each other in the jungle and gossiping about who might fancy who. On the next night, they watch youngsters who are locked in a house together, hoping they might decide to have sex or at least a row.

At times, it's so bad it makes you think that it must have been better to live in a time when families gathered round a piano singing hymns at night. At least life was real then, not like the so-called reality TV shows.

The worst thing about these types of programmes is they stop us thinking. I see it all the time in my family: my brother watches TV all the time and is becoming a vegetable. My sister is so addicted to 'Friends' that life for her stops between 8pm and 9pm. I'm glad I can escape to my room and read a book!

Contrast: explains what he dislikes most; note the exaggeration for effect.

powerful image

Explains problems with evening TV.

Second problem explained.

Why he does not like the programmes – words like 'gossiping' show he is critical.

Explains why we act as we do.

'because' introduces the reason.

sarcasm

Explains it is the unreality of reality TV shows that he dislikes.

'the worst thing … is …' shows he is about to give a reason.

Shows how this affects his family, and why it upsets him.

Conclusion: sums up criticism.

Good Points

- The introduction introduces two features of TV which he dislikes.
- The two main dislikes are then explained in detail in separate paragraphs.
- The answer concentrates on 'why' and 'how' rather than just 'what'.
- The language is entertaining in places (e.g. 'the soaps drip on and on'), and includes sarcasm.
- There is a good attempt to vary sentence structure.

Task

Explain how you have dealt with difficult situations that have arisen in your life.
You might wish to write about:
- relationships with parents
- friends and their expectations
- problems at school
- any other difficult situations you have met.

Writing to describe

Key points

- One of the questions in Section B of Paper 2 lets you **write to describe**.

- You will probably have to describe a **person or place**.

- When writing to describe, you should:
  - describe what you know
  - plan and structure the description
  - write an effective introduction and conclusion
  - use your five senses, as appropriate
  - go into detail.

Top Tip!

The aim of descriptive writing is to give the reader a clear picture of the person or place you are describing. It is very unlikely that you will be asked to write a story.

Describe what you know

- Describe something or someone **you really know about**. You may think it is more interesting to describe someone from Siberia, but your lack of knowledge will show in the writing.

- If you invent a **person**, base them on someone (or some people) you know well. He or she will then come across as a real person.

- If you are describing a **place**, choose one where you have lived, or one you have visited.

Structure

- **Group your ideas** together in a plan. Unless you plan carefully, your description will ramble and have no structure.

This is a **plan** for a response to the question: 'Describe a beach in August.'. The main ideas have each been given a separate paragraph. The further details show how the ideas can be developed.

PLAN

Intro:
the overall atmosphere on beach

Para 2: families
dads red, mothers looking after babies and youngsters

Para 3: children
on sands, in sea, ice cream, sunburn

Para 4: sea
sandy grey waves, seaweed, lilos

Conclusion:
view from the pier, people drifting to steps and home

Good Points

- The plan is clearly divided into sections.
- Some ideas for developing the main points are given in each section.

Introduction

- A **lively opening** will immediately attract the examiner's attention.

> When I arrived at the beach, it was busy and exciting. Families in bright T-shirts were packed together, music blared and children were screaming. The sun beat down and the waves lapped against the shore.

Grade C

Top Tip!

For a really striking opening, think about a different approach, e.g.
- Focus on one family in detail.
- Focus on one particular area, then broaden out.
- Begin with someone speaking.

Good Points ✓

- It is clear from the start what the student is writing about.
- Sounds, as well as sights, are described.
- The beach and the people are both described.
- Interesting words are used ('packed', 'blared', 'lapped').

Include all five senses and detail

- Good descriptive writing usually appeals to **all five senses**. Write about what you (or other people) are seeing, hearing, touching/feeling, smelling and tasting.

- The more **detail** you include, the better the description. Describe a particular beach towel, for example, not just beach towels in general.

Note how this extract uses the techniques above.

Top Tip!

If you are writing a description of a person, don't include all the senses. Instead, try to include some description of background, such as the things they like to do.

sight

taste

feeling

> The coloured windbreaks and T-shirts were bright. You could smell sun-tan cream and fried onions from hot-dog stalls, and your lips tasted of salt and sand. All along the beach, the fathers sat in deck chairs, reading their newspapers with sweat running down their necks or lay on towels. The mothers tried to make the children behave properly, shouting at boys and girls, who were shouting back. One woman in a Liverpudlian accent was screaming, and looked set to explode.

Grade C

smell

sound

Top Tip!

Good descriptive writing often includes features that are found in poetry. For example, you could include a simile such as 'fathers sat in deck chairs, going red like apples in the sun'.

Good Points ✓

- All the senses are used to help the reader experience the seaside.
- There is some good detail, such as 'fried onions from hot-dog stalls'.

Conclusions

- Your conclusion should **round off the writing**. Don't let it just tail off.
- Try to **link** your final paragraph in some way with the introduction. Go back and read the introduction before you write your conclusion.

Look at how this student ends her response:

'Now' shows that we have moved on to a different time.

Shows how the people are moving away.

> Now, it is cooler in the evening sun. The sand is mixed with litter and the sandcastles are broken down. Families are heading home. They queue at the steps to leave the beach. The children are tired and quiet, and parents carry bags and towels. The tide is coming in again, and soon it will be cleaning all the mess away.

Grade C

Shows how the beach has changed.

Hints at what will happen soon.

Good Points

- A good description, which describes the weather, the beach and the people.
- This final paragraph links effectively with the introduction: time has moved on.
- Details show how things have changed, e.g. the children are quiet now.

Using a range of techniques

Try to use all the techniques dealt with in this section, as in the answer below.

> Describe a person who inspires you.

Contrast makes an effective introduction.

> Some people choose sportsmen or soldiers as their heroes. However, the person who inspires me is not famous, he goes to the same school. His name is Jonathon and he is paralysed from the waist down.
>
> Before he was injured he was very well built – and according to most girls, he was the Brad Pitt of Year 11. He was captain of the football team and Head Boy of the school. Then, just before his mock A levels, he went downhill on a sledge in the snow and hit a tree. When he woke up, he was in the serious injuries unit in Stoke Mandeville Hospital, and was told he might never feel any movement below his neck again.
>
> He did, though. He wanted so badly to get better and be mobile. He did not want to be looked after for the rest of his life. He had too much living still to do.

Grade C

Description of his looks and abilities

Detail – name of hospital makes it real.

Description of his attitude – note short sentence for surprise effect at start of paragraph.

Describes his intelligence.

Conclusion returns to the idea of being an 'everyday' hero.

humorous simile

> Now, he goes round in his wheelchair like a racing driver and does wheelies all the time at parties. Although he's missed so many months, he's going to pass all his exams with A grades, and should get a good university place. He might not ever be able to play rugby but he will make an excellent doctor, which is what he wants to do.
>
> He must lie awake at night and be very upset. Still, his arms are becoming stronger, he wants to complete a wheelchair marathon and convinces you that he will do it. He will not accept his life has been ended by being in a wheelchair.
>
> Because of all this, Jonathon is greater than Wayne Rooney or Neil Armstrong or anyone else I have ever heard of. He is so normal, but also so different. He convinces you that he can do anything he sets his mind on and he's a great inspiration to us all.

Top Tip!

When describing someone, you usually give your own views. You could add variety and interest by including:
- a conversation with them – to highlight how they talk or think
- someone else's view of them.

✓ Good Points

- The response is well structured. Each paragraph describes a different aspect of Jonathon.
- Some detail and interesting words are used.
- Clear sentence structure with some powerful short sentences for effect.
- There is an effective introduction, which is referred to in the conclusion.
- The writing shows the student's feelings about Jonathon.

Combining types of writing

- An option in Section B for both Papers is to write a response which involves more than one kind of writing. For example:
  - A question on Paper 1 might ask you to argue, persuade and advise.
  - A question on Paper 2 might require an answer that describes and explains.
- Any combination of writing skills is possible. You can use the skills you have learnt for each type of writing to cover all the types of writing that the question is asking for. For lots of practice questions, you can use the *Exam Practice Workbook* which starts on page 97.

Task

Describe a place where you spend much of your time, for example:
- a park
- a swimming pool
- a club
- your bedroom.

Raising your grade

Key points

If you want to raise your grade to C or above, you need to show these skills. All extracts are from a response to the question on the right:

> Write an article for a national newspaper in which you argue that parents should or should not be held responsible for the actions of their children.

Purpose and audience

- Think hard about the **purpose** and **audience** of the task before and during writing.
- For example, if the **purpose** of the task is to argue or explain, don't inform or describe.
- Make sure the **form** of the writing suits the purpose, e.g. a letter, speech, advice leaflet.
- Think about the **audience** – what kind of language and style would suit them?

> It is crazy that parents should be punished if their sons or daughters truant from school. After all, when someone becomes a teenager, they know what they want to do – and they do it, whatever their parents say.

Clear argument shows a strong sense of purpose. The formal style suits the audience (newspaper readers).

Structure and planning

- Make sure you do a **plan** before you begin writing.
- Use **paragraphs** to organise your writing: a new paragraph for each new point or idea.
- **Develop the points** in your paragraphs, and use words like 'however' and 'next day' to connect them.

> Mind you, some people say that if children are brought up properly, there won't be a problem and it's down to the parents from the start. But it's not as simple as that ...

New paragraph to present the opposing argument. 'But...' shows how the next idea counters this.

Make your writing more exciting

- Grab the **reader's interest** and keep it, for example by using quotations, anecdotes (stories), examples and humour.
- Use **interesting vocabulary** wherever you can. Go back and change words when you are checking your work.
- **Vary** the length and structure of your **sentences**. Use different kinds of sentence (e.g. questions, exclamations).

> Imagine, for example, how a parent might have to struggle if a 16-year-old refuses to go to school. What is the mother supposed to do? Does she stop his sweety money? Of course she can't.

Variety of types of sentence, and lengths of sentence. The questions get the reader's attention. 'how a parent struggles' is more interesting vocabulary than 'what a parent does'.

Punctuation, grammar and spelling

- Use **punctuation** to control your sentences.
- Make your **grammar** as accurate as you can.
- Try to spell accurately.

> You can bring your kids up really well, but if they make some bad friends they are led astray easily, like when they are out on the streets.

Note the commas used to separate the parts of the sentence.

Read the question and an extract from a student's answer below.
The notes show why the examiner awarded it a C grade.

> We usually know most about those closest to us. Write a **description** of a member of your family.

Links to what has gone before.

Grade C

> However, when he was younger, he was very different. You can see it in old photographs and my father has told me a lot about him. He was wild and used to go round with gangs of 'rockers', as they were called. Sometimes he would get into fights. Once he even ended up in hospital.

Punctuation used accurately: here, inverted commas.

Keeps up the interest by adding detail.

> He used to ride an old motorbike that was always breaking down and he would get home late and covered in oil. He never seemed to mind though, and perhaps that is why he eventually ended up opening the garage and working there all hours of the day and night.

Quotation brings character to life.

> He is happy there. As he once said to me; 'Where else can you mess around with engines and get covered in mess and get paid for it? It's brilliant.' That is how he sees the job and because he enjoys it so much, lots of people take their cars to him to be fixed. He is a very popular mechanic.

> At home, he spends a lot of time in the garden. That's not because he likes gardening, it's because my Auntie Sylvia makes him go out there, to get him out from under her feet. He spends a lot of time in his shed and we aren't sure what he does there really . . .

different types of sentences

humour

Purpose is clear throughout: tight focus on uncle.

- The response gives a clear picture of the man. It is in an appropriate style for the audience – in this case, the examiner. There are attempts to engage the reader's interest, for example the quotation and the touch of humour in the final paragraph. The paragraphs are well linked and the writing is mostly accurate.

Answers

Remember that there are no 'right or wrong' answers in English, as there are in Maths or Science. The answers below are only examples of Grade C responses. Compare them with your own answers: if yours contain similar features, then you are working at Grade C level. If your answers don't seem as good, then ask yourself how you can improve them.

page 9

Grade C

The first text relies heavily on opinions, for example 'Sharon's going to cause a lot of trouble' and she is called 'mouthy'. These opinions make us think badly about Sharon even before we have seen her: they turn us against her but also make us interested in watching. And this is why the opinions are given, because the purpose of the text is to make us watch the programme.

The second text, by contrast, begins with facts. Because it is a newspaper report, it sets out exactly what is happening: who is collecting money and why. The report ends by printing the facts about the problems of Africa: over 2 million killed because of AIDS, and so on. This is probably to get people to donate money. The opinions in the article come from Graham. He talks about the 'unfair world' and 'injustice'. He says, 'the problems … are hard for us even to imagine,' which is of course his opinion.

In conclusion, the texts are very different, but each suits its purpose. The *Inside Soap* article is mainly aimed at advertising a TV programme so it talks it up. The newspaper article is mainly aimed at reporting factually what Graham and Chris Lingard are doing, and his opinions are part of the story.

page 13

Grade C

The writer fears he is becoming old. He used to like *Top of the Pops* and Tony Blackburn, and now pop music on TV is full of 'semi-naked girls'. So the way things have moved on is really what he is writing about.

He begins by telling you something about himself, so that you know how old he is and how he is a bit worried about this. He is looking forward to watching pop music with his children, but 'shock and dismay' it is totally different now. The son is cool about this but he is horrified, he realises he is heading towards the last stage in his life and even thinks about bingo and stair lifts. At the end he pulls himself together and realises that he must appreciate what he's got now 'while I still can'.

The writer uses lots of techniques to get you on his side. Humour is one, for example 'No drier in the toilets?' And it is funny how he gets so stressed out by the Kiss channel but his son is cool about it. This is also an example of contrast, which he uses a lot as well, for example the *Top of the Pops* DJ was 'friendly, reliable, old', as opposed to the 'semi-naked girls faintly disguised as pop artists'. He also exaggerates a lot, like when he says pop stars have rings all over them like chain mail.

page 17

- **exaggeration**: All eyes turn to the sea
- **simile**: like a satellite
- **direct address to reader**: you'll find
- **list**: Sorrento, Positano, Salerno and Amalfi
- **metaphor**: fleeing across
- **simile**: statues sit like sentinels surveying

page 20

Each column begins in the same way, first with a quote, to show the most important thing that the person thinks about the question. For example the cleaner's quote is 'I work hard because I have no choice'. This is a harsh view of life, which contrasts with the two quotes of the other two people interviewed.

page 23

Grade C

The report comes from a popular newspaper and is against the arrival of the ship. The headline says it is 'a toxic rust-bucket', which turns the reader against it immediately. The word 'protest' in the strapline adds some human interest by showing that it is something that people are up in arms about. The language is powerful throughout the article, for example a 'rusting ghost ship' and 'packed with toxic chemicals'. We aren't just given the facts but there is opinion too. And because the final paragraph is a quote from a protester, we are left with that point of view.

The report is very short, with just one sentence in each paragraph, which makes it easy to read. There is far more space given to the photo and the headlines. There are two headlines and the second one is underlined to make it stand out. The picture is huge to show that the ship is a massive problem, and it looks deliberately old and grey and dangerous. People are shown on the shore, though hardly the crowds mentioned in the article.

Grade C

The first text does have some facts, such as that Crossley had his first teaching post at Loveridge Primary School, but most of it is opinion. It consists of Crossley telling a story about how he got the attention of the class. When someone is telling a story from long ago you cannot tell how truthful it is. And it includes a lot of exaggeration, such as 'nervous wreck' and 'transfixed'.

Text 2 is different because it is full of facts. The first sentence tells us the facts that Frank is 78 and that he lives on the Albany Estate. Later on it gives details of what the gangs have done to him. However, some of the words used make us feel strongly about the situation, such as 'prisoner in his house'. This is the opinion of the writer, who could have said 'Frank hasn't wanted to leave his house'. Also, Frank's own opinion is given at the end.

The two texts have different audiences, which explains why their use of fact and opinion is different. Text 1 is read by teachers who want to hear a lovely story. Text 2 is from a newspaper, so people want the facts above all, but they also want to feel strongly about the story, so there are opinions as well.

Reading poems from different cultures and traditions

page 29

There are no 'correct' answers: any two poems are acceptable, as long as you have a clear idea about how they both focus on the theme in the question. All the poems below come from the first eight poems of the Anthology (Cluster 1), but you can compare poems from either cluster in your exam answer. The following list is just a starting point for your revision.

<u>Suffering</u>
Limbo – slavery
What Were They Like? – contrast between peaceful life and war
Others possible: *Night of the Scorpion, Blessing, Nothing's Changed*

<u>Poverty</u>
Night of the Scorpion – family living conditions
Blessing – lack of water
Others possible: *Nothing's Changed, Two Scavengers in a Truck*

<u>Inequality</u>
Nothing's Changed – contrasts between whites and blacks
Two Scavengers in a Truck – totally different lifestyles
Other possible: *Limbo*

<u>Man and Nature</u>
Vultures – linked through love and evil
What Were They Like? – what the war did to the country
Others possible: *Blessing, Night of the Scorpion, Island Man*

<u>Contrasting cultures</u>
Island Man – differences between past and present
Two Scavengers in a Truck – the rich and poor
Others possible: *Nothing's Changed*, any contrast between the cultures presented in the poems

page 31

Extract from a Grade C response

… The society we see in *Two Scavengers in a Truck* is one that is in parts. On one side there are the scavengers, but they are on a garbage truck and they are separated from the richer people:

> 'looking down into
>
> an elegant open Mercedes'.

The gulf between them and the rich is significant. Both sets of people are at the same stop light but have no real connection – the couple in the elegant car do not even seem to cast a glance at the poorer scavengers.

We see a similar society in South Africa in *Nothing's Changed*. There, the whites have a smart new restaurant: 'new, up-market, haute cuisine', while the poor blacks have to make do with a 'working man's café'.

In this case, we do not see the whites with the advantages, but we learn about the world in which they live, which has:

> 'ice white glass,
> linen falls,
> the single rose'.

This is made to appear very beautiful, and is a contrast to the world of the working blacks:
> 'wipe your fingers on your jeans,
> spit a little on the floor:
> it's in the bone.'

The poet is speaking sarcastically. If people behave badly, it is because of the conditions. Probably the scavengers do not want to look 'grungy' either, but in both cases they have no real choice: this is their life, whilst others have all the advantages …

page 35

Extract from a Grade C response

The poem is set in a hot country, where the people are poor and there is little water. When the pipe bursts and water shoots out, they become excited and rush out to collect it in anything they can. The children play in it, though.

The poet has sympathy with these people. She understands that they are always short of water:

'There never is enough water.'

She describes the effects, as 'skin cracks like a pod'. She shows how they dream of water: 'Imagine the drip of it'. She describes it in religious language (e.g. 'kindly god', 'blessing'), which shows it is important to them. In fact, the water is seen as 'fortune', 'silver' and 'liquid sun'. It is very valuable.

The message of the poem is that sometimes things can be better. Yes the people fight for the water but that's because of how desperate they are. The children are happy when the water 'sings' over them. Though we finish with an image of their 'small bones' which makes us think they are weak and it won't be long before there is no water again.

Yet this is still much more positive than the message in *Not my Business*, because here the suffering has no break. It reveals endless violence in a society. Dharker sees the problem as one of climate and a lack of water, but Osundare sees the problem in evil people.

page 37

Extract from a Grade C response

The poem is set out in two sections. The first section has a series of questions about the people of Viet Nam. The second section answers them. The questions suggest the Vietnamese are artistic people – or rather were, because it suggests that so many have been killed. For example:

'Did they use bone and ivory,
jade and silver, for ornament?'

The answers are unpleasant – for example, 'Sir, their light hearts turned to stone'. Each answer shows how their life and culture were destroyed: 'Sir, laughter is bitter to the burned mouth.'

The poem moves towards the final ending of death – 'It is silent now.' This is because their culture, traditions and happiness have all gone.

So the poem has a strange structure but the reason is to make the reader remember all the good things about life in Viet Nam before the war. Then the answers show how the terrible war has affected the country. The structure is effective, because the questions describe a beautiful world, where the Vietnamese are happy, then the second section shatters this dream. Also, it's like someone asking the reader questions, so it's direct.

page 41

Extract from a Grade C response

Dharker begins with metaphors of hatching ('breaking out' and 'cracking'), which suggests new growth. There is then a list of open things: 'space, light, / empty air'.

The words suggest things going upwards, and the sound effects such as the use of 'c's emphasises the amazing scene. The climax is 'crash through clouds'.

Alvi, though, is describing a life where she is stuck. She contrasts the softness of the Pakistani clothes ('satin-silken') with the more basic British clothes she really desires: 'denim and corduroy'. The presents are more exotic but she explains in a simile she 'could never be as lovely as those clothes'. She feels out of place between two cultures. She wants to rise out of it like a phoenix (a mythical animal that grew out of the ashes) but cannot.

Dharker's poem is positive, with lots of images of moving upwards and getting brighter. Dharker's life is being re-born, but Alvi is not like a phoenix, she is trapped and she does not seem able to rise out of her frustrating life: 'my costume clung to me'.

page 45

Grade C

Both *Half-Caste* and *from Search For My Tongue* are about people who are uncomfortable in the society where they live. John Agard is angry, because he does not feel 'half' of anything, Sujata Bhatt is worried because she thinks she is losing her mother tongue, through speaking English all day.

Agard demands an explanation for the way people speak to him: 'Explain yuself'. Calling him 'half-caste' is insulting. Because he does not want to be seen as 'half-caste', he gives examples of how colours are mixed – painting and music and weather. Since none of these items are thought of as half-caste, why should it happen to him?

Agard is sarcastic:

'Excuse me
standing on one leg
I'm half-caste'.

He is making fun of those who label him, he demands they come back as whole people to see him:

'wid de whole of yu ear
and de whole of yu mind'.

They are the ones who are not proper, complete people. Then, he says, they will learn he is a whole person:

'an I will tell yu
de other half
of my story'.

These final lines are in a stanza on their own, to make them stand out and show how angry the poet is. The poem is about his bitterness about the idea of 'halfness'. The poet deliberately doesn't use much punctuation and use of common speech patterns, but we are meant to notice how intelligent he is too, as he talks about art and music, and his use of long words like 'consequently'.

Bhatt's problem is that she is uncomfortable handling two languages, which represent two cultures. Since she speaks in a foreign tongue she thinks her mother tongue could die. She believes it dies and rots, and she spits it out and thinks she is left with only the new language.

Since she uses the metaphor of a flower to talk about her language, it shows she thinks it is delicate and beautiful. Then she reveals that the tongue, like a plant, grows back in the night. It seems to be the better language, because she says 'it ties the other tongue in knots'. She sounds delighted at the end, when the mother tongue 'blossoms'.

Bhatt's feelings, like Agard's, are also shown successfully. Her mother tongue is used in the poem to show the reader what she dreams (in Gujerati). This shows us how difficult it must be to live with a difficult second language. How relieved Bhatt is when her tongue survives is cleverly shown as it grows from a rotten leftover, to a stump, up to a bud, then a flower which blossoms. The poem begins with her unhappiness at having lost her tongue, but ends with her recovering it.

Writing

page 51

1 the text of a speech (form/purpose)
your year group (audience)
inform (purpose)
what the school offers out of lesson time (content)

2 For example:

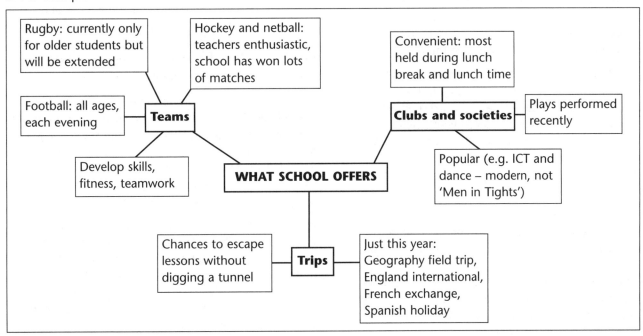

page 55

Castle World is your once-in-a-lifetime chance to go back in time. You can be a knight for a whole day, or you can be a servant in the fabulous great hall. The amazing rides and activities are so stunning that you will want to stay in the Middle Ages instead of going home.

page 57

At home, Uncle Tom seems to spend countless hours locked in his study. This isn't because he enjoys marking mountains of school books … no, it's to escape from the dreaded Aunt Sylvia. Another escape route is school, 3 miles down the road, where he often works late into the evening.

page 59

1 Jake's guitar teacher rang. He said he's going to a gig in Birmingham.

2 "It's hopeless, isn't it?" she sighed. "All the socks are muddled up."

page 61

except – means 'to leave out'. Correct word: accept

arguement – argument

exsessive – excessive

disapear – disappear

sychologicle – psychological

affect – effect. 'Affect' is the verb, 'effect' the noun.

doesnt – doesn't. Always remember to include
   necessary apostrophes (see page 58).

ocasionaly – occasionally

choclate – chocolate

definately – definitely (stem word: finite)

vegatables – vegetables

losts – lots (presumably a careless error)

improof – improve

ourselfs – ourselves

page 65

Grade C

Bolton is not the worst place in the world, but it is not the best place either. It has a premiership football team and is close to motorways, so it is easy to travel around. However, if you are sixteen, you want more things to do and Bolton does not really have them.

I like to dance and mix with my friends. I also love ice skating. It is not possible to do either of these activities easily, though, because we are not provided with meeting areas like handily placed youth centres or ice rinks. It is hardly surprising we do so badly in the Winter Olympics. Many people agree with me and feel that the local council should apply themselves to giving us more of what we want.

A good youth centre, for example, would get teenagers off the streets and into doing something more worthwhile. As well as letting us let off some steam in the evening, the centres could organise trips out to other places nearby, so we could try different sports, play against other towns and cities and so on. They might even take us to the coast in the summer or to the countryside in the winter.

Having these opportunities would change many youngsters' attitudes. It might mean they would feel more positive about where they live and they might be more willing to contribute to charities and things like that. Instead of mugging little old men and stealing cars, they could sit in comfortable surroundings and drink coffee and tell their friends what is wrong with their lives. Parents would be happier too, knowing that their sons and daughters are safe.

So, I would say to all you readers that it is worthwhile to ask for more entertainments and centres to be provided. If we all put the council under pressure, I think they will change their policies and make Bolton an even better place to live. I am already proud of my town. If we all work together, we can make it even better.

page 69

Grade C

In Britain, we are living in a society that has a lot of money and where nobody needs to starve. People are paid well and most people have a job. Not everyone is living in a perfect state, but most of us have a roof over our head. It is easy to forget that not everyone is as lucky.

In the Third World, many people live very poor lives. They have to work all day for not much money and they cannot afford decent food or houses. Charities like Oxfam and Action Aid help them to help themselves, but we need to support the charities if they are to do that. An organisation like Water Aid only needs a small amount of money from each of us each month and they can provide wells and clean water. Can you think of a better cause? You should help them if you can.

What is more, even in England and Wales, some people still need support. There are some old people all on their own. The Salvation Army can help them. And there are drug addicts on the streets, with nowhere to turn. If we raise money for the charities that help them, we are doing our bit for our own society too.

It does not take much to be some kind of hero. My friend Katie did some fund-raising by doing a sponsored skip. We all thought she was crazy, but she managed to raise £85, which she gave to the St Mungo's Appeal, and will have made some poor people very happy over Christmas. You can even do a sponsored run, or hold a bring and buy sale. Every little helps.

It is better still if you get involved by helping to run the charity or actually care for others or deliver food parcels or even man the telephones. Doing work like that is better than sitting at home watching *EastEnders* or some reality show with second rate celebrities on it. If you help, you will be a real star, not just someone who wants to be more famous.

page 73

Grade C

Dear Miss Knowles,

Now that we have got the extra money from the government, I am writing on behalf of Year 11 to tell you what we think you should do with it. £100,000 is a lot of money, and we think that if it is spent properly, there will be many benefits for the whole school.

We would like you to consider spending it in different areas – to improve the sports facilities, the computer room and the library. However, we also think the students would like some rest and recreation areas. We have some classrooms that are not often used. We would like to see those developed so we can use them as common rooms at break and lunchtime.

The sports hall needs new equipment for gymnastics, volleyball and so on. If a chunk of the money is spent on improving it, the standard of fitness in the school might improve, which would be a good result. If more of the cash is spent on the dry play area and the fields, goalposts and cricket nets, then there is no doubt the school's sports results would improve too. That would help the school's reputation.

The computer room needs more printers and new mice, because students keep pinching the balls. Also, the library needs re-stocking and should have magazines each week, because that would encourage more students to go in there. Hey presto, our exam results would then start improving too.

Then, if we had common rooms as well, we would be out of the rain and better able to concentrate in lessons and we would not be hanging around outside in the cold. It would not cost much to provide drinks machines – which might even pay for themselves – and some games, like pool and darts boards. The students would then be much more positive about school and behaviour would improve.

So you see, if you spend the money in these ways, the school will be a much better place. We hope you take our ideas seriously.

Yours sincerely …

page 77
Grade C

I love playing badminton. Once I have finished my homework each evening, I go straight down to my local sports hall. I am allowed to play badminton for as long as I want, provided no one else is waiting for a court. This is because I am a member of the Arnside Racquets Squash and Badminton Association.

I started to play when I was just six years old. My mum says I could always hit the shuttle but it did not usually go where I wanted it to. By the age of twelve, I was playing for the junior team and now I represent the seniors. I sometimes play singles when we have matches, and I am always in the doubles team.

We play matches all year round, because in our area there is no real 'season' for our sport. This means that once a month, on average, I play a home match and once a month I play away. That is always even more fun, because all the players in the team get on really well, and we have a laugh together. Once they even threw me in a swimming pool when we won our last

match and avoided relegation. I think it was because I had done well, not because no one likes me.

I have won quite a lot of trophies. I was second in the county two years ago, in my age group, and have played in the national championships. Unfortunately I was knocked out early on. I had a cold and did not do well. Anyway, in my bedroom there are twelve shields and some certificates framed on the wall. That is not to be big-headed, just because they inspire me to try even harder in the future.

Since I am so involved in badminton, I have little time to do anything else. My dad always says that isn't a problem, so long as I am enjoying what I do. My ambition is to play for England, and for Great Britain in the Olympics, and he approves of that, so I'll just keep on practising. I think that he is hoping I'll be able to get him lots of free tickets for the finals – but I just want to wear the team's track suit and win a gold medal.

page 81
Grade C

Everything that goes wrong for me seems to be connected to my friends. If there is a problem at school or at home, I have to sort it out by getting my friends sorted out first. That is just the way it goes.

Take getting to school on time. I always get up early, but then my mates come round to the house late, so we get to school late. I get into trouble from my parents if the school gives me detention, so I have to try to talk to my friends and make them understand what is happening. I even end up going to school on my own sometimes, when they look like letting me down. On occasions, I might have to grab a lift from Marcie who lives next door, and I don't like her parents at all. That's how serious it is.

My friends also used to get me into trouble when we were out at nights. Once or twice, the police were involved. It came about because we were hanging around the old people's bungalows, and they hated it because they thought we were going to break in and steal all their Abba CDs or throw bricks through their windows. Anyway, my parents made my life a misery again and grounded me for about a million years, so I told my friends we had to find a new place. Now, we usually have a laugh just down the road from the police station, which is quite ironic, really.

The worst problem I have ever had, though, was when I got a really nice girlfriend called Suki, and she said I had to choose between my mates and her. She didn't like them. She said they were a bad influence. One night she just said, "All right, what's it going to be?"

I've never liked being told what to do, so I said I was just going to do what I felt like. That sorted out the problem straight away, because she left and I haven't been out with her again.

Overall, I believe I can deal with problems with my friends and can usually sort things out without making situations worse. Now, my friends are becoming more sensible all the time, so there are less likely to be problems in the future.

page 85

(Grade C)

Most of my life out of school is spent in the local park. That might not sound very interesting, but the park is where all my friends meet, and it has different parts, because it is so big. We can play around in the adventure playground, with its skateboard section; we can play football on any of the fields, or in the arena. We can have a laugh at people on the pitch-and-putt course; or we can just frighten the ducks down by the lake.

Sometimes, when we are on the rides and swings, we must look like young children again, but we don't care. There's a slide that's about ten metres high, there's a roundabout that turns us into a blur, and a brilliant rocker that takes eight of us. We throw it forwards and back and you can hear the girls screaming at the other side of the park.

We go on the pitches too, but they are always full of mud which oozes over your trainers and makes the knees of your jeans stick to your legs. Of course, at weekends the nets are up and teams pour into the park to play league matches. There are blues and reds and whites everywhere, and people chanting.

At weekends, too, we hang around the pitch-and-putt course, because it's even funnier than the bowling greens. Many of the old men playing bowls are actually quite good, even if they do all wear flat caps, but the pitch-and-putters mostly haven't any idea at all. On sunny days, there are kids running around pushing golf balls ahead of them (thirty hits to get to the green), women swinging and missing and men smashing the bushes about trying to find their missing ball. It's brilliant.

I know that the park seems like a strange place to spend all your time, but it's better than just watching television and it's not all the same. In fact, when the fair comes in summer and it's full of frying onions and rides, it's one of the best places in the world.

Index

Collins

Collins Revision

GCSE English

Exam Practice Workbook

FOR AQA A

Written by Keith Brindle

How to use this workbook

How this workbook is organised

This exam practice workbook is designed to help you develop your exam skills and test how well you are doing. Hopefully, it will show you are 'on the right lines' as well as pointing out some areas that you might be able to improve.

It deals with the final exams only because your coursework has to be completed before the exam period.

It links closely to the pattern of the AQA A GCSE English exam:

English Paper 1	Final exam: 1 hour 45 minutes	Section A: 1 hour Reading media and non-fiction texts 15% of final marks	Section B: 45 mins Writing to argue, persuade, advise 15% of final marks
English Paper 2	Final exam: 1 hour 30 minutes	Section A: 45 mins Poems from different cultures and traditions 15% of final marks	Section B: 45 mins Writing to inform, explain, describe 15% of final marks
Coursework	Produced during the course	4 written assignments 20% of final marks	3 speaking and listening assignments 20% of final marks

There are five major sections in the exam practice workbook:

Paper 1: Reading media and non-fiction texts (pages 100 – 123)

Paper 2: Poems from different cultures and traditions (pages 124 – 161)

The skills required for Section B (Writing) responses (pages 164 – 173)

Paper 1: Writing to argue, persuade, advise (pages 174 – 181)

Paper 2: Writing to inform, explain, describe (pages 182 – 189)

As you work through the book, you can check how well you have done by referring to the Answers further on in this book or by visiting **www.collinseducation.com/easylearning**. Here you will find full mark and grade guidance given in a **free** easy-to-download format.

How to use this workbook

Work through the tasks provided in the different sections and then mark your own work to find how well you have done. This will test your ability to respond to the requirements of each part of the exam.

Paper 1 Section A: Reading media and non-fiction texts

The same skills are tested in the exam each year, so you can aim to maximise your performance by practising the essential skills. The exercises allow you to check how well you can follow an argument, comment on presentational devices, and so on.

Paper 2 Section A: Poems from different cultures and traditions

There are double pages on each of the set poems, so both Clusters are included. There is a final section which gives the opportunity to practise the skill of comparing poems, using exam-style questions.

Skills for Section B responses

The Writing skills for both papers have much in common so you can practise planning, writing effective openings and endings and using high quality features such as quotations and anecdotes, as well as a range of punctuation and functional skills.

Paper 1 Section B: Writing to argue, persuade, advise

You have the opportunity to deal with each kind of writing in the triplet, as well as combining their requirements, in the sort of question that blends these forms in the exam itself. At the end of each section, there is another title for you to tackle, to help you improve your performance.

Paper 2 Section B: Writing to inform, explain, describe

This section follows the same pattern as the previous one, but focuses on the forms of writing which feature in Section B of Paper 2.

Paper 1 Section A: Reading media and non-fiction

Responding to the questions

Section A of Paper 1 should take you one hour to complete. The exam paper will contain two or three texts. You will have to read them and then answer questions on them. There are likely to be just two questions broken into smaller parts so you will probably have to offer four, five or six answers.

The questions will focus on the following assessment objectives:

(i)   read, with insight and engagement, making appropriate references to texts and developing and sustaining interpretations of them;

(ii)   distinguish between fact and opinion and evaluate how information is presented;

(iii) follow an argument, identifying implications and recognising inconsistencies;

(iv) select material appropriate to their purpose, collate material from different sources, and make cross-references;

(v)   understand and evaluate how writers use linguistic, structural and presentational devices to achieve their effects, and comment on ways language varies and changes.

These may seem very difficult and confusing but they mean that when you examine the texts, you will be writing about how the writers:

* use fact and opinion
* construct their argument
* use language
* use presentational devices and, possibly, structure.

You are also likely to have to say how successful the writers have been; and will probably have to make a comparison of some kind between the texts. You will be expected to support your ideas with appropriate references. This means that whatever you say should be linked to the purpose and audience of the texts.

Although nothing is absolutely certain, the first set of questions might be about fact and opinion, argument and the texts' purposes and audiences. The second set of questions is likely to focus on the media aspect of one text or both texts and you will probably be asked to write about presentation and language in that part.

When answering the questions, you should consider the following advice:

1 Notice how many marks are available for each question, and use your time appropriately. You should spend about two minutes per mark, since there are 27 marks for Section A

2 Look closely at the question and make sure you are producing exactly what is required. Do not just write about the texts in general terms. If necessary, underline the important words in the question, so your attention is focused

3 Offer evidence for any ideas you give, either by referring to something in the text or by quoting directly. Remember that the PEE technique (point/evidence/explanation) is the best approach.

The paper will look like this:

Paper 1 consists of two sections. Only Section A of the exam paper is given here.

Paper 1 Section A: Foundation Tier

In addition to this paper you will require:
* Text 1: *Need a break? Want a change? Why not try Bognor …?*, from a weekend magazine
* Text 2: *Ancient art of relaxing*, from the *Sunday Express*

These are the texts that you will be given in full in the exam. They are both media texts. They are not reproduced here.

READING: NON-FICTION AND MEDIA TEXTS

Answer all the questions in Section A.
Spend approximately 60 minutes on Section A.

Remember to spend up to 10 minutes of this time reading the texts carefully, before answering the questions themselves.

This question is asking you to identify the purpose and audience of Text 1 – not to write about the text in general.

1 Re-read Text 1: *Need a break? Want a change? Why not try Bognor …?*

a) What is the intended purpose and audience for this text? Give your reasons.   *(5 marks)*

b) How does the writer try to convince us of his argument? Explain:
   * the main points of his argument
   * how fact and opinion are used
   * how other techniques are used.   *(9 marks)*

This refers to any persuasive techniques that the writer uses, such as anecdotes, statistics or humour.

This question is asking you to show how well you can follow, and evaluate, the argument. Make sure that you cover all the bullet points in your answer.

2 Next, re-read Text 2: *Ancient art of relaxing*.

a) Why have the presentational devices been included? To what extent are they appropriate for the text?   *(5 marks)*

Finally, compare the two texts.

b) How does each writer use language?   *(8 marks)*

Total: 27 marks

This question is asking you to think about the use of such devices as headlines, photos, graphics, bullet points, use of colour and design and to comment on their effectiveness.

Note how many marks are awarded for each question, and allocate your time accordingly.

The final question usually asks you to compare the texts. In this case, you are being asked to compare only their use of language. To compare, you will need to use material from both texts, and make cross-references between them.

Purpose and audience

Why are purpose and audience important?

You might be asked to write about the purpose and audience of a particular text.

If that does not happen, the purpose and audience are still key considerations, because each element of the texts you will be looking at are chosen for a particular purpose.

Purpose

1 Why has the writer written this text? You might wish to offer alternative ideas but try to support what you say with quotations from the article.

_____

_____

_____

_____

_____

_____

_____

_____

_____ *(4 marks)*

Hero beats the Atlantic – now for GCSEs!

Michael Perham is fourteen years old but has his name in the record books. He sailed single-handedly across the Atlantic, alone for six whole weeks. He faced gales, 25 foot waves, danger from larger ships, loneliness and sharks. But back on dry land, he now has to face the ultimate test: his GCSE examinations.

Michael seemed very calm after arriving in Antigua, and was looking forward to returning to his home in Hertfordshire. However, the small matter of GCSE exams stand between him and his next voyage, a non-stop round-the-world trip he is planning.

He has a great deal to do before he can set out again. After all, he only took some RE work with him this time, yet did not find a moment to start on that, even with six watery weeks on his hands. He might well be a hero to his classmates, but his teachers will just see him as someone who needs to catch up!

Michael on his yacht, sailing back to his studies.

Sunday Times, 21.01.07

Audience

2 Below, there are some extracts from texts. Say:

- who you think they were written for
- why you have come to that decision.

Extract	Audience	Reason for decision	Marks
'For the woman in your life: "Erotique", the new fragrance by Henri.'	————	_____ _____ _____	2
'Throughout the nineteenth century, nurses continued to do as they were told by doctors. They knew their place.'	————	_____ _____ _____	3
'Discipline your children. No longer can they be allowed to do exactly as they wish.'	————	_____ _____ _____	3
'Investors in Sun Life Assurance of Canada rejoiced earlier today, as share values reached unprecedented heights.'	————	_____ _____ _____	3

Audience and purpose

3 What is the purpose of this text, and how does it appeal to its audience?

_____
_____
_____
_____
_____
_____
_____
_____
_____
_____
_____
_____
_____
_____
_____

Continue on lined paper if necessary.   *(6 marks)*

Selecting relevant information

What information do I have to select?

In Section A of Paper 1, you are being tested on your ability to locate precisely the right details to answer the questions correctly. You might have to comment on the information as well.

Read this report.

> Tiny Stanningly Village has never seen a night like last night – and may never do again!
>
> For a top rock band to agree to play for an audience of just 100 people is unusual enough. For such a band to play for free, for nearly two hours, is probably unprecedented. Yet that is what Silver Snake did, last night, on the Stanningly village green. And it was all designed to help a little girl enjoy the final days of her life.
>
> When Silver Snake heard about seven year-old Jodie Graham, who has terminal cancer but adores the Snakes and their music, they got in touch immediately. The concert was planned in matter of days. Jodie, her friends, family and neighbours were all invited whilst the remainder of the village could just sit in their garden and listen as well!
>
> 'They were fantastic,' said Jodie. 'It's been a dream come true.'
>
> For the Snakes, their manager, Chrissie Hallett, said, 'The guys heard about Jodie, and were pleased to do all they could. She's a great little kid.'
>
> The manager chatted to Jodie for an hour and presented her with a signed copy of the band's latest CD, T-shirts and posters.
>
> 'They have brought joy into her heart,' said Jodie's mum.

1 List five things that made Jodie's life happier.

_____

_____

_____

_____

_____

_____

(5 marks)

2 What detail in this report might suggest that the band could have done more?

_____

_____

_____

(2 marks)

This is a letter, sent to a newspaper, about a young man who was shot as a deserter in the First World War.

It is difficult to find words to express my sadness at the attitudes of the villagers of Shoreham who feel unable to include the name of Private Jack Brown, shot for desertion, on their war memorial.

Brown was a boy of 19 when he experienced the horrors of the battles of Mons and Le Cateau in World War I. Many were sent insane by the experience. Private Brown cracked and ran away.

I was on active service at the age of 18: I didn't undergo 1 pc of this lad's experience, but I'm not ashamed to admit that I was scared when I was fired on. Only a fool would not be. The desire to run away becomes over-whelming in any normal human being.

So, Shoreham, put this boy's name on your memorial. Let him at last rest in the peace he deserved.

P SMITH, Maidstone, Kent

3 What do we learn about Private Jack Brown? Write down four facts.

_____

_____

_____

_____

_____

_____   *(4 marks)*

4 What sort of person is writing the letter? Quote to prove what you are saying.

_____

_____

_____

_____

_____

_____

_____

_____   *(6 marks)*

This is another letter on the same topic.

Some of those executed during World War I were guilty not of desertion, but of murder and rape. Others had already been warned for disobeying orders or neglecting their duties.

Without a painstaking examination of every case, we run the great risk of putting such people's names on war memorials alongside those of heroes who conquered their fear and died doing their duty.

B JONES, Bournemouth, Dorset

5 In your own words, say why this writer has a different viewpoint.

_____

_____

_____

_____

_____

_____   *(4 marks)*

Developing interpretations

What does this mean?

Think about moving beyond the obvious and try to decipher what a writer is trying to say about a person or a situation. This development becomes clearer as you link ideas and possibilities.

This is a programme preview from a television magazine.

Little Britons in the Sun

Benidorm : ITV

A couple of years ago, I went on the worst holiday of my life – a package deal to Turkey for about the price of a pint. It was the week of 9/11, but the holidaymakers in Marmaris seemed unfazed. As long as they could tan their skin red, take full advantage of the all-you-can-eat buffet, and drink themselves into oblivion, all was well. I might have thought *Benidorm* was the stuff of fantasy had I not experienced Marmaris.

This new comedy is set in the Solana resort in Spain. Not that it makes any difference, as no one moves from the pool. Here, going abroad is not about the experience of a new culture. It's about bringing Britain with you.

All the usual suspects are here – family from Hell, complete with racist, chain-smoking granny, middle class couple who couldn't be any less enamoured with their surroundings, or indeed, each other, pub quiz champion and his mother. My 'favourites' are Jacqueline and David, the husband and wife who enjoy crosswords.

In places, this is very funny. But there's also something deeply depressing about *Benidorm*, which has more to do with the subject matter than the quality of the writing. There are those within Britain who are fairly intolerant of cultural differences. Rather than laughing my way through the programme, I found myself thinking that these kinds of holidays might go some way to explaining (though not excusing) some racist behaviour we witness. If going abroad means actively seeking segregation from other cultures, perhaps the traditional British package holiday is more damaging than we realise.

Nicole Jackson
The Observer Television Magazine, 01.02.07

1 What worries does the writer have about package holidaymakers?

Make close reference to the text in your answer.

_____

_____

_____

_____

_____

_____

_____

_____

_____

_____

_____

_____

(5 marks)

This is an extract from a longer text.

Even amongst those who knew him well and might call him a friend, Anthony Jaggers was a person to be handled with care. According to the movie director who set out to chart Jagger's life, the man was simply evil. Those who did not have the luxury of escape across the Atlantic have usually been more guarded in their assessments, though many regarded him with absolute terror.

Strange, then, that someone like Miranda Stanbridge should speak fondly of him after his death. To hear her obituary for him, you might think the man had spent much of his life in church and all his spare time working for charities and the environment. On national television, she spoke of his kindness and compassion.

Had she misjudged him totally; or were there two sides to the man once labelled 'The Dark Avenger'?

There can be no doubting the fact that he attended church regularly, though whether that influenced his life for the better is less sure. Similarly, he was seen at charity events in the Home Counties, but the size of his contributions to good causes has never been revealed. He was also a loving son to his mother, who doted on him. She seems to have overlooked the fact that he was imprisoned in the 1970s for battering to death his cousin, who was just fifteen at the time ...

2 To what extent does the writer balance the different views of Jaggers' personality?

_____

_____

_____

_____

_____

_____

_____

_____

(4 marks)

3 What do you think is the writer's opinion of the man, and how is it made clear to the reader?

_____

_____

_____

_____

_____

_____

_____

_____

_____

(4 marks)

Fact and opinion

Is it enough to be able to spot facts and opinions?

No. It is almost certain that you will have to write about *how* facts and opinions have been *used* by the writer. You might, for example, be asked to find two facts and two opinions and say how they support the writer's argument and whether the argument is convincing.

This is an extract from a blog produced by a scientist based in Antarctica.

22 December

We are all working hard and checking temperatures, air quality and the thickness of the ice on a regular basis. However, with Christmas approaching, we seem to have a little more spare time, and I have been able to enjoy some of the delights that this incredible white expanse has to offer.

I've been out on a boat, and a huge pod of Orca whales swam past. Fantastic! I've even seen young elephant seals sunning themselves through the day, and Weddell seals and some nesting skuas, which fly at you if you go near. The penguins are just crazy: and I mean they are not very bright at all. On land, they rush towards you, then panic when they notice you are not a penguin, and try to run away and fall over. Yesterday, one of the stupid birds actually leapt out of the sea and into our boat for a few seconds. Then he shook his head and leapt back into the waves. Maybe he had thought we were a taxi?!

The best thing yet has been our transparent glacier ice. We brought it back from a trip to see some small crevasses that are opening up on the glacier. It's not like normal blue glacier ice. We keep it in the fridge and put it into our drinks. Imagine having ice that is thousands of years old with your gin and tonic ...

1 Find five facts about what the scientist has been doing and five opinions that show his attitude towards what has happened.

Facts	Opinions

(5 marks)

2 What is the scientist's attitude towards her life in the Antarctic? How does she use facts and opinions to show her attitude?

_____

_____

_____

_____

_____

_____

(6 marks)

Continue on lined paper if necessary.

This is an article from a magazine.

Jennifer Aniston: happier than ever!

People keep feeling sorry for Jennifer Aniston – but goodness only knows why. 'Tragic Jen' or 'poor Jen' seems to be how the media see her: yet we have to ask why. She is a beautiful, talented multi-millionairess; seems to have recovered remarkably quickly from her two splits from Brad Pitt and Vince Vaughn; and, surely, won't be single for long.

Approaching 40, she looks as good as ever, and the world's favourite ex-*Friend* is still one of the hottest properties in show business. She has much to thank the show for. She was paid an incredible million dollars an episode for the later series, has been nominated for an Emmy five times and been on the cover of *Vanity Fair*. And then there is her hair: it makes the world's hairdressers go weak at the knees.

She has, recently, appeared in a number of movies, and TV shows, to rave reviews (*Friends with Money*, *The Break-Up*, *Dirt*), has been talking about adopting a baby boy, following the lead of Angelina Jolie, and must, surely, be looking for a new and more lasting partner. 'I don't make plans,' she says – but the woman who has regularly topped polls for the 'world's sexiest' must have pretty limitless options.

As far as she is concerned, as long as she is happy, that is all that matters.

Sunday Express Magazine, 28.01.07

3 How are facts and opinions used to create a positive image of Jennifer Aniston? Is the writer successful in her aim?

_____

_____

_____

_____

_____

_____

_____

_____

_____

_____

_____

(8 marks)

Follow an argument

There will always be one question that requires you to read through a text and show you understand how the writer has put across the argument. You are likely to have to explain the main points and write about the techniques used in the text, for example, the use of contrast, quotation, examples and so on.

Read this extract.

Last night, I was re-reading …

Isn't it incredible how so few educated people refuse to admit they read so little? 'What do you think of Plato's *Republic*?' you ask them. 'Oh, very grand, very grand …', they reply. Of course, if you ask what they found grand about it, they make a rapid exit. Almost certainly, they have never even used the book to stand their coffee on, never mind as late-night entertainment, as they sip their hot cocoa. But why don't they just say: 'I've never read it. When I do read – mostly on the beach – I prefer books with lots of killing/romance/humour/romping in. Philosophy is deadly'? Because they would feel shown up, that's why. Life is too competitive, even when you leave the playground.

There seems no end to the pressure, because those who do read regularly over-state their qualities. Instead of 'I've just been reading *The Da Vinci Code* and …', they regale us with: 'I was <u>re</u>-reading it recently and …' Intellectual snobbery again – 'I am better than you because I read more, <u>and</u> re-read extensively.'

This is all so strange. Yes, we should read to enrich our lives; but what is there to brag about? Like those who give to charity or secretly eat Smarties in front of *Casualty* every Saturday night, we should keep our private life to ourselves. There is nothing wrong with recommending a book that has given you great pleasure, but never sneer at those who prefer *Coronation Street* or *Eastenders*. They too have their wisdom.

A friend of mine is a doctor and the way ardent readers peer down their noses at him frustrates him greatly. He has always loved the sciences but to be accepted in so much society he is expected to have a close working knowledge of literature and the arts. 'I am supposed to have read all the great novelists and poets,' he sighs, 'but my friends who studied English at University are not expected to know how to transplant kidneys, or to quote the latest research statistics dealing with Alzheimer's disease. The world isn't logical.'

Indeed it isn't. But I tell him it would be better if only Plato were in charge. He nods, and tells me the *Republic* is a grand book.

1 What is the writer saying about our attitude to reading? Explain in your own words, but quote to prove your points.

_____

_____

_____

_____

_____

_____

_____

_____

_____

_____

_____

_____

_____ *(6 marks)*

2 How does the writer make the argument convincing and interesting?

Write about:

- the opening
- the ending
- the range of techniques the writer uses.

_____

_____

_____

_____

_____

_____

_____

_____

_____

_____

_____

_____

_____

_____

_____

_____

_____

_____ *(8 marks)*

Language

Don't we deal with language when we are looking at poetry?

Yes, but there will also be a question about the language used in at least one of the unseen texts. Obviously, you cannot analyse the whole text, so try to focus on the most striking examples of language usage: perhaps a simile, a metaphor, a short sentence, complex phrasing etc. Always say what effect is being created, and why.

Below is the opening paragraph from a review of Shakespeare's *The Tempest*. It has been broken into sections. Examine each part, saying what is interesting about the language used.

1 Let's face it, modern productions of Shakespeare are not always everyone's cup of tea.

_____

_____

_____

_____

(2 marks)

2 Last night's performance, at the Grand Theatre, left most of the audience wondering whether they should have stayed at home and watched even *Big Brother*; because there you have control and can switch off if you wish. In the privacy of your own home, you are safe from the modern directors who deal with the Bard's verse as if it were a rejected script for *Eastenders*, to be spat out, rushed and mutilated – obscene and best not heard.

_____

_____

_____

_____

_____

_____

(3 marks)

3 Nothing was as it should be. Prospero, Shakespeare's final great creation, was perverse and perverted; Ariel was deranged; Caliban was hideously naked.

_____

_____

_____

_____

_____

(3 marks)

4 (This was a set of foul freaks. Shakespeare's last play deserves better.)

_____

_____

_____ *(1 mark)*

Read this extract.

What never fails to astonish me, on my travels, is the behaviour of young people abroad. How can it be that teenagers who have never come anywhere near a school uniform have not turned into mass murderers? Why aren't they drunk all the time? Why aren't they like young people in Britain?

British schools work so hard – but with what success? It's like trying to cork a bottle of beer: pushing, forcing squeezing, just to see everything spill over. The government insists on 'higher standards', and head teachers wield their metaphorical rods of iron, yet when the school gates are unlocked and the children tumble out, the neighbourhood has to be braced.

First, there is likely to be the tugging and name-calling. Bustle and noise. Then the ball games, smokers, shrieks ... And later comes the alcohol, some drugs ... Passing the local park can be as dangerous as passing the pub doors at 11.00 pm, when the elder siblings leave the bars and head for the takeaways and taxi ranks and more disputes and nights in the cells.

If it doesn't happen in France, Italy, Portugal, Greece, why does it happen here?

5 How is language used by the writer?

_____

_____

_____

_____

_____

_____

_____

_____

_____

_____

_____

_____

_____

_____ *(6 marks)*

Structure

What will be asked about structure?

You might be asked about how a text has been put together and/or why particular features have been placed in a particular order or position.

1 Re-read the text on the previous page. How does the writer structure the passage?

_____

_____

_____

_____

_____

_____

_____

_____

_____

_____

(6 marks)

2 This advertisement is aimed at teachers looking for promotion. How has it been structured?

Write about:

• the order in which you notice things, and why

• the order of the details in the text.

_____

_____

_____

_____

_____

_____

_____

_____

_____

_____

_____

_____

_____

_____

(6 marks)

Bridlington School Sports College

Bessingby Road, Bridlington, YO16 4QU

Headteacher

L31-35 • NOR 1050 • Sixth Form 117

We are looking for higher achievement
   ...with change already underway
      ...a new senior leadership team
         ...a changing culture

You will join us to
   ...fuel the vision
      ...drive the progress
         ...and ensure success

We seek a visionary leader who will lead a talented and committed team; someone who can use the skills of others and is clear thinking and decisive.

Whilst the school has enjoyed a good reputation for many years, it was placed in Special Measures in February 2005.

This is therefore a unique opportunity to have a special impact on the school and its future.

You will have knowledge and understanding of what constitutes good learning and teaching, a commitment to inclusion and the "know how" to develop a highly successful school.

This position becomes vacant in September 2007.

Application pack available by telephoning (01482) 391205 or online at www.recruiteastriding.co.uk

Post No: BRIDSSCHTS. Closing Date: 23 February 07. Interview Date: 15 & 16 March 07.

This council is pursuing equality of opportunity in employment.

FOR MORE JOBS: www.recruiteastriding.co.uk

EAST RIDING

OF YORKSHIRE COUNCIL

Education Guardian, 06.02.07

Look at this newspaper extract.

BEATLEMANIA

£500m-a-year bonanza as Fab Four set to go on download

EXCLUSIVE

By GRAHAM BROUGH

THE Beatles are poised for a huge revival after a deal yesterday paved the way for their songs to be downloaded for the first time.

iPod makers Apple Inc settled a 28-year trademark battle with Beatles record company Apple Corps over the use of the name.

It means massive hits such as Hey Jude and Yesterday may soon be legally downloadable – sparking a wave of Beatlemania worth £500million a year.

FULL STORY: PAGE 10

PLAY JUDE
We give classic Beatles album cover the iPod treatment

Daily Mirror, 06.02.07

3 How is it structured to gain maximum impact?

_____

_____

_____

_____

_____

_____

_____

_____

(4 marks)

Presentational devices

What are presentational devices?

This term covers items such as photographs, diagrams, text boxes, headings and sub-headings. You will be expected to explain how these devices have been used in the text. There will always be a question about presentational devices.

Read this newspaper extract.

Sunday Mirror,
28.01.07

HOW TECHNOLOGY COULD HELP

One idea is to use aircraft to pump reflective dust into the atmosphere to block sunlight

Scientists have suggested sending giant mirrored dishes into orbit to reflect sun's rays

Let's block sun with smoke and mirrors

Rapped... Exxon site

AMERICAN experts have come up with a bizarre solution to global warming and climate change – putting giant mirrors in orbit round the earth to bounce sunlight back into space.

They also want to use jet aircraft to pump reflective dust into the atmosphere and send up thousands of shiny balloons to block sunlight.

The US wants the radical ideas adopted by the Intergovernmental Panel on Climate Change (IPCC) as "insurance" against rising levels of carbon emissions and other greenhouse gases, for inclusion in a long-awaited UN report.

Scientists reckon reflecting less than one per cent of sunlight back into space could make up for man-made greenhouse gases over 400 years.

Meanwhile Esso's owners ExxonMobil – the world's biggest oil firm – were yesterday accused of peddling climate-change propaganda to schoolchildren on a website it funds. MPs say the Energy Chest site featuring "Joules the Robot" questions whether global warming is man-made.

Lib Dem spokesman Chris Huhne MP branded the firm's bosses "Toxic Texans" and "climate-change deniers". He added: "ExxonMobil is behaving in a thoroughly irresponsible manner, doing itself and its shareholders no favours by failing to recognise reality."

1 Read the text, then explain how the presentational devices:

- attract the audience
- support the article.

_____

_____

_____

_____

_____

_____

_____

_____

_____

_____

(6 marks)

Look at this advertisement.

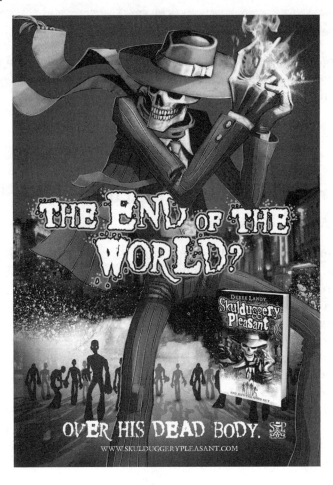

2 How are presentational devices used in this advertisement?

_____

_____

_____

_____

_____

_____

_____

_____

_____ *(4 marks)*

3 What different effects would be achieved if the background colour were:

- orange
- silver?

_____

_____

_____

_____ *(2 marks)*

Making comparisons

You will have to compare some part or parts of two texts. This is something you do in Paper 2, when you compare poems (see pages 158 – 161); but you are also likely to have to make comparisons in Section A of Paper 1.

You might be asked to compare any aspect of the texts.

JAMES MORRISON ON EATING, DRINKING AND £1000 A HEAD MEALS

When you're a musician, you flip between eating stuff to just fill you up, or eating at amazing restaurants. Before I got signed, I was taken to a few posh restaurants by different labels. There was one, called Silks, where the bill was over £1000 – £30 for a bottle of beer! I went to get one at the bar and they were like, 'we'll get it.' I was like, 'thank God'. I'm not from a very privileged background, so any food I can eat, I'm glad of. Last year on tour I had incredible sushi in Tokyo and amazing soups and fried prawns in Holland. But our rider used to be just sandwiches and beer – before I'd really sold any records it was cans of Carling. Then we got Becks. Now we get Corona! Selling a million albums means on the next tour I'm getting backstage catering. A roast now and then would be brilliant.

I could cook a roast but I burn most stuff. My mum came up from Cornwall recently, and cooked this Moroccan dish – bulgar wheat, lamb and red wine. She's an amazing cook; we never had lots of money but she made sure we had great meals.

I don't drink before a show. Beer's bad for your voice – the bubbles give me claggy stuff in the back of my throat. Or I get gassy. It's all right for Liam Gallagher, but that's his style, isn't it?

The Observer Food Monthly, 01.07

WaterAid UK site

Water-related diseases kill thousands every day

Access to water is a basic human need and a fundamental human right. Yet one in eight people in the world still live without safe, clean water to drink.

Millions of women and children spend hours every day walking miles to collect water. But, the water they work so hard to collect doesn't come from a tap – but will come from a river, pond, or simply from dug out holes in the ground, often shared with animals and polluted with waste and excrement. The diseases that result kill 5000 children every single day.

Known and feared round the world, **cholera** is an acute intestinal infection spread through contaminated water.

While **giardia** normally produces a mild bowel infection, its effects can be much worse in developing countries, leading, in some cases, to death.

Rotavirus causes severe diarrhoea and vomiting and is estimated to kill around 600,000 children under five every year in developing countries.

Around 200 million people worldwide are affected with **bilharzia**. This parasitic worm penetrates the skin. Fever, malaise, nausea and diarrhoea follow with liver failure and even death if left untreated.

Despite the clear need, water and sanitation are not high on the political agenda. They are almost so obvious they are forgotten.

WaterAid website

Compare the texts on page 118 by answering the following questions.

1 How does each text deal with drinking?

_____

_____

_____

_____

_____

_____ *(2 marks)*

2 What are the purposes and audiences for these two texts?
Explain your ideas.

_____

_____

_____

_____

_____

_____

_____

_____

_____

_____ *(4 marks)*

3 Compare the use of facts and opinions in the texts.

_____

_____

_____

_____

_____

_____

_____

_____

_____

_____

_____

_____

_____

_____

_____ *(6 marks)*

Skills test: Paper 1 Section A

Yes. Remember to produce answers of an appropriate length and to refer to precise detail wherever possible to support your ideas.

Write your answers on lined paper.

Read both texts carefully and then answer all the questions.

Spend about an hour on your responses.

Text 1: An article from a national newspaper

Need a break? Want a change? Why not try Bognor ...?

According to government figures, 5.5% of the UK's carbon dioxide output comes from aviation fuel. Air travel is feeding our destruction. At the same time, with global warming all too apparent, Britain is getting pleasantly warmer whilst southern Europe is falling into the grip of heatwaves that look set to kill thousands. Catastrophic water shortages will no doubt be next. Under the circumstances, it is hard to work out why it is that millions of Britons take to the skies each year, seeking rest and some form of relaxation. It would be so much more sensible to stay at home.

For centuries, the lure of the exotic has been tempting, but now we have seen it all. Television in the 21st century brings Ancient Rome, the Steppes, even the lunar landscape into our living rooms. What more is there to see? Simultaneously, the Mediterranean is becoming increasingly polluted, the beauty of backwaters is being overwhelmed by MacDonalds, and it is no longer cheap to live in Spain or Greece.

The bargain days are over. It costs relatively little to get abroad – in terms of cash, and if you forget the ozone layer – but, having arrived, you are back to grim reality. Bread and milk have to be paid for.

Meanwhile, Britain retains its history, its glorious beaches (think of Croyde in Devon, the vast stretches in Northumberland, Morar in the Highlands) and its charm. Nothing on the continent has more mystery than Stonehenge. Staithes in North Yorkshire is every bit as fascinating as Hydra in the Aegean, and to get there does not require a choppy sea crossing on a boat long ago deemed unsafe to work across the Channel. It is as easy to be pampered in Bognor as it is in the Bahamas. A night out in Manchester offers as much as Berlin or Munich.

Flights abroad will have to become a thing of the past if the world is to survive. Our future summers will have to be spent in our green and pleasant land, but that is no great loss when the whole of Wales opens its arms and thousands of hidden nooks around our coasts are waiting for us to call. As Hamlet would have put it: 'Tis a consummation devoutly to be wished.'

Ancient art of relaxing

After a hard day's sightseeing in Athens, there is no better place to be than the Hotel Grande Bretagne. JANE MEMMLER checks in to soothe her weary limbs.

ACROPOLIS NOW: Take in heady views from the hotel's rooftop restaurant

MANY VISITORS to Greece bypass Athens, its dusty capital, and head straight to the islands. What they're missing is a place with a wealth of history and fabulous shopping. So take a detour and spend a few days in this frenetic yet exhilarating city.

If you're looking for class, look no further than the Hotel Grande Bretagne, one of the world's classic hotels. Its location, right on the city's central Syntagma Square, is perfectly placed for exploring the old area of Plaka and Monasteraki and is close to Athens's defining monument, the Acropolis. The imposing Parliament buildings are directly opposite and worth a visit just to see the guards in their funny pompom shoes and flared skirts.

At the Grande Bretagne, prepare to be overwhelmed. Grecian columns, miles of marble and ornate gilt furnishings make you feel as if you've stepped into an old palace.

Passing through the revolving doors come dozens of men in suits, ladies in crisp business-wear and heels and the odd casually-dressed tourist. The smart liveried doormen hardly bat an eyelid and are eager to help you find your way.

Best of all, are the views from the roof. Sweeping across to the Acropolis and the old Olympic Stadium, at night these illuminated landmarks are truly spectacular against the twinkling lights of Athens.

THE ROOM

Continuing the theme from the lobby, the rooms are grand yet cozy. A large ornate mirror, elegant table lamps and highly-polished bureau make up the busy, yet uncluttered room. Heavy swathes of Regency

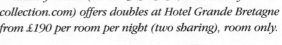

CALM WATERS: The pool area provides a sea of tranquillity

curtains, in burnt gold and claret, give the room a Louis XVIth feel. The beds are covered in crisp linens and have loads of squishy pillows. The bathroom, in true Grecian style, is clad in floor-to-ceiling marble, with a large shower and luxuriously deep bath.

THE SPA

The award-winning GB spa is a tranquil respite from the hustle of Syntagma Square. Comfortable white sunloungers are lined up along white marble walls surrounding the pool. Individual relaxation areas are scented with uplifting essential oils.

My therapist, Dimitri, who had the hands of a god, bathed my feet before giving me a body massage. When I showered it off, I'd felt as if I'd been cleaned by a tube of toothpaste.

THE NOSH

There is a selection of restaurants to choose from within the hotel. You can push the boat out in GB Corner on the ground floor with such dishes as oven-baked shrimps with pan-fried grouper to something a little lighter in the rooftop bar and restaurant, such as grilled steaks and salads, while you soak up the views of the sprawling city.

THE DAMAGE

EasyJet (0905 821 0905/www.easyjet.com) offers return flights from Gatwick to Athens from £52.

Luxury Hotels (00 800 3254 5454/www.luxury collection.com) offers doubles at Hotel Grande Bretagne from £190 per room per night (two sharing), room only.

Sunday Express, 28.01.07

Re-read Text 1: *Need a break? Want a change? Why not try Bognor ...?*

1 a Why does the writer think it is good to take holidays in Britain? Answer using your own words. *(6 marks)*

b Which do you think are the writer's best two points, and why? *(2 marks)*

c How does the writer try to make us agree with him?
Write about:
- the uses of fact and opinion
- other techniques he uses to make us agree with him. *(6 marks)*

Now, re-read Text 2: *Ancient art of relaxing.*

d Who do you think this text has been written for? Explain your opinion. *(4 marks)*

Finally, look at both texts together.

2 How do the texts try to interest the reader?
Write about:
- each writer's use of language
- presentational devices in *Ancient art of relaxing*. *(9 marks)*

(Total: 27 marks)

Re-read Text 1: *Need a break? Want a change? Why not try Bognor ...?*

1 a What is the intended purpose and audience of this text? Give your reasons. *(5 marks)*

  b How does the writer try to convince us of his argument?
  Explain:
  • the main points in his argument
  • how fact and opinion are used
  • how other techniques are used. *(9 marks)*

Next, re-read Text 2: *Ancient art of relaxing.*

2 a Why have the presentational devices been included? To what extent are they appropriate for the text? *(5 marks)*

Finally, you must compare the texts.

  b How does each writer use language? *(8 marks)*

(Total: 27 marks)

Paper 2 Section A: Poems from different cultures and traditions

How to respond to the questions

Section A of Paper 2 should take just 45 minutes to complete. The exam paper will offer you a choice of two questions. You will have to answer one of them.

One question will be on the first Cluster of poems:

- *Limbo* – Edward Kamau Brathwaite
- *Nothing's Changed* – Tatamkulu Afrika
- *Island Man* – Grace Nichols
- *Blessing* – Imtiaz Dharker
- *Two Scavengers in a Truck, Two Beautiful People in a Mercedes* – Lawrence Ferlinghetti
- *Night of the Scorpion* – Nissim Ezekiel
- *Vultures* – Chinua Achebe
- *What Were They Like?* – Denise Levertov

The other question will be on the second Cluster:

- *from Search For My Tongue* – Sujata Bhatt
- *from Unrelated Incidents* – Tom Leonard
- *Half-Caste* – John Agard
- *Love After Love* – Derek Walcott
- *This room* – Imtiaz Darker
- *Not My Business* – Niyi Osundare
- *Presents from my Aunts in Pakistan* – Moniza Alvi
- *Hurricane Hits England* – Grace Nichols

Each question will name a poem from the Cluster. You choose one poem to compare with it.

The poems are all from different cultures and traditions, so you will be expected to write about those cultures in your response. However, that need not be a concern for you because by answering the question that is set, you will automatically write about the cultures and traditions in the poems.

You will be marked according to how well you respond in writing in these three areas:

1 the ideas, feelings and attitudes in the poems
2 comparisons, including appropriate details from the poems
3 the presentation in the poems: language and structure.

Make sure you are including these features as you answer the question.

The practice questions in this book focus on the ideas and the presentation. There is a separate unit to allow you to compare the poems.

There are different ways in which you can write your essay in the exam. You should always begin with an **introduction** which demonstrates how you will answer the question. Rather than just repeating the question, try to say something about the poems and how you intend to deal with the task:

> I am going to compare Presents from my Aunts in Pakistan with another poem of my choice and say what we learn about the people in the poems and how the poets present their ideas. ✗

> In Presents from my Aunts in Pakistan, we are introduced to a girl who is torn between two cultures. The poet reveals to the reader what is in the girls' mind and her apparent unhappiness. However, in Hurricane Hits England the situation is slightly different ... ✔

In the **main body** of your response, you might choose to compare the poems by writing about their comparable features. Or, you might respond to one of the poems in detail and then deal with the second, pointing out ways in which it compares with the first one at that point.

Either:

Method 1:   point from Poem 1/ point from Poem 2, as comparison
            point from Poem 1/ point from Poem 2, as comparison and so on

or

Method 2:   all points from Poem 1 then points from Poem 2, making comparisons with Poem 1 as you go.

Finally, add a **conclusion** which sums up the main points you have made.

Throughout, you should be using the **PEE** technique:

- make your <u>point</u>
- give an <u>example</u> to prove it
- <u>explain</u> your idea.

As with any other element in an exam, the more you practise these techniques, the better!

Limbo
by Edward Kamau Brathwaite

What is the poem about?

Like all the poems from different cultures, it presents a cultural situation to the reader. In this case, it centres on slaves being transported to America. It tells of their suffering and has the rhythm of the limbo dance. The ending could be interpreted as optimistic or pessimistic.

1 What is happening in the poem?

_____

_____

_____

_____

_____

_____

_____

_____

_____

_____

(6 marks)

2 What effect is created by these lines:

> *stick is the whip*
> *and the dark deck is slavery* ?

Comment in detail on the words used.

_____

_____

_____

_____

_____

_____

_____

_____

(4 marks)

3 Why is there a repeated refrain:

> *limbo*
> *limbo like me ?*

_____

_____

_____

_____

_____ *(3 marks)*

4 How are rhythm and rhyme used in the poem?

_____

_____

_____

_____

_____

_____

_____

_____

_____ *(6 marks)*

5 Is the ending optimistic or pessimistic?

Make your opinion clear by referring closely to:

- the final section (from line 40 onwards)
- the rest of the poem.

Try to refer in detail to the language and structure of the poem.

_____

_____

_____

_____

_____

_____

_____

_____

_____

_____

_____

_____ *(8 marks)*

Continue on lined paper if necessary.

Nothing's Changed
by Tatamkhulu Afrika

Do I have to know about South Africa to understand the poem?

It is enough to be aware of the fact that there used to be a system called apartheid in South Africa, where the white people were in charge and considered themselves superior. In the poem, apartheid has ended and Tatamkhulu Africa revisits District 6, an area which black people had been forced to leave.

1 How does the reader react to the opening stanza?
Write about:

- the words used
- how the words are organised in lines.

_____

_____

_____

_____

_____

_____

_____

_____

_____

_____   *(6 marks)*

2 Why does the poet make the comparison between the _'whites only restaurant'_ and the _'working man's café'_?
Include:

- details of the comparison
- an explanation of the effect that is created.

_____

_____

_____

_____

_____

_____

_____

_____

_____

_____

_____   *(6 marks)*

3 How is the poem structured?
Consider:

- the order in which ideas are placed
- how the order gives structure to the poem.

(4 marks)

4 What do we learn about the feelings of the poet?
Write about:

- his anger and how it is shown
- the ending of the poem.

(10 marks)

Island Man
by Grace Nichols

Will we be expected to write about such a short poem?

This poem is relatively short and it simply captures the moment when a man wakes up. However, there are important points to make about his background and his emotions, as well as the contrast between his home in the Caribbean and his life in London. These points offer much to consider.

1 What happens in the poem and how does the man feel about it?

_____

_____

_____

_____

_____

_____

_____

_____

_____

_____

_____

_____

_____ *(6 marks)*

2 How is the contrast between the Caribbean and London presented?

_____

_____

_____

_____

_____

_____

_____

_____

_____

_____

_____

_____

_____ *(6 marks)*

3 Comment on the effect of the following:

the steady breaking and wombing	
he always comes back groggily groggily	
Comes back to sands *of a grey metallic soar*	
island man heaves himself *Another London day*	

(6 marks)

4 Why are the opening and ending of the poem appropriate, considering the poet's message?

_____

_____

_____

_____

_____

_____

_____

_____

_____

_____ (5 marks)

5 How do the layout and punctuation of the poem contribute to its message?

_____

_____

_____

_____

_____

_____

_____

_____

_____

_____ (5 marks)

Blessing
by Imtiaz Dharker

How religious is this poem?

The poem presents a third world country in which the people are poor and water is scarce. When the municipal pipe bursts, it is like a miracle and is seen by the poet in religious terms. The people, of course, are elated.

1 How is the lack of water shown at the start of the poem?

(5 marks)

2 How are the ideas of religion brought into the poem?

(4 marks)

3 Which words show the value of the water? Explain their effect.

(3 marks)

4 Why is there such a long sentence to end the poem – beginning *'From the huts ...'*
(line 11) and ending *'over their small bones'*?
Write about:

- how the mood of the people is shown
- the language used
- the punctuation
- the stanza break.

_____

_____

_____

_____

_____

_____

_____

_____

_____

_____

_____

_____

_____

_____

_____

_____

_____

_____

_____   *(10 marks)*

5 Why is the title of the poem appropriate?

_____

_____

_____

_____   *(2 marks)*

Two Scavengers in a Truck, Two Beautiful People in a Mercedes by Lawrence Ferlinghetti

What is there to say about the culture in this poem?

What happens in the poem probably seems very close to our own experiences because it is set in America. However, the experience is one that is tied by the poet directly to America and it is presented as something with particular significance within that culture.

1 What do we learn about the garbagemen?

_____

_____

_____

_____

_____

_____

_____

_____

(5 marks)

2 What do we learn about the *'elegant couple'*?

_____

_____

_____

_____

_____

_____

_____

_____

(5 marks)

3 How are the two sets of people contrasted?

_____

_____

_____

_____

_____

_____

_____

_____
_____
_____
_____
_____   *(6 marks)*

4 Why is the poem set out as it is on the page?

_____
_____
_____
_____
_____
_____
_____   *(3 marks)*

5 What is the message at the end?
Comment on:

- the ideas
- the language used.

_____
_____
_____
_____
_____
_____
_____
_____
_____
_____
_____   *(6 marks)*

Night of the Scorpion
by Nissim Ezekiel

What is different about this poem?

Unlike most of the poems, this one offers a narrative. As well as an impression of the culture, we are also given the story of what happens when the poet's mother is stung.

1 What sort of narrative technique does the writer use?

_____

_____

_____

_____

_____

_____

_____

_____

(4 marks)

2 What are we told about the setting of the poem?

_____

_____

_____

_____

_____

_____

_____

(3 marks)

3 In what ways is the structure of the poem effective?

_____

_____

_____

_____

_____

_____

_____

(4 marks)

4 What do we know about the people who try to help the mother?
Write about:

- what they do
- what they say
- how language is used to show what they are like.

(12 marks)

Vultures
by Chinua Achebe

Will we be asked about this poem, when the language is so difficult?

You are allowed to pre-prepare poems in the Anthology, which means the question could be about any of them. If this poem seems particularly tricky, you need to have an overview of what it is about and you must be able to write about the different sections.

1 In your own words, explain briefly what each section of the poem is saying.

_____

_____

_____

_____

_____

_____

_____

_____

_____

_____

_____

(6 marks)

2 What is the mood of this poem, and how is it created?
Consider:
- the opening of the poem
- any other details that you find relevant
- the long sentences.

_____

_____

_____

_____

_____

_____

_____

_____

_____

_____

_____

_____

_____

(10 marks)

3 How are we supposed to feel about the vultures?

(6 marks)

4 How are we supposed to feel about the Commandant?

(4 marks)

5 What is the poem telling us about love?
Quote to support your ideas.

(6 marks)

What Were They Like? by Denise Levertov

Will we be asked about the structure of this poem?

You will never get a question just about structure. However, you will want to explain how the poem is structured because that is likely to be relevant to almost any answer on this poem.

1 How is this poem organised, and why?

_____

_____

_____

_____

_____

_____

_____

_____   *(4 marks)*

2 Why does the poet include: *'Sir ...'* ?

_____

_____

_____

_____   *(2 marks)*

3 What does the poet suggest life was like before the war?

_____

_____

_____

_____

_____

_____

_____

_____

_____

_____

_____

_____

_____

_____

_____

_____   *(8 marks)*

4 How are peace and war contrasted in the second section of the poem?

_____

_____

_____

_____

_____

_____

_____

_____

_____

_____

_____

_____

_____

_____

_____

_____   *(10 marks)*

5 How does the ending affect the reader?

_____

_____

_____

_____

_____

_____

_____

_____   *(5 marks)*

from Search For My Tongue
by Sujata Bhatt

Is the whole poem metaphorical?

It is all based around an extended metaphor. In this way it deals with ideas about cultural identity, how the poet copes in another country and who she really is.

1 What is the main message in this poem?

_____

_____

_____

_____

_____

_____

_____   *(4 marks)*

2 *'I have lost my tongue'* introduces the central image. How is it extended through the poem?

_____

_____

_____

_____

_____

_____

_____

_____

_____

_____

_____

_____

_____

_____   *(8 marks)*

3 Why is the Gujerati included?

_____

_____

_____

_____   *(3 marks)*

4 Consider the style of the poem. How does the reader become involved in what the poet has to say?

_____

_____

_____

_____

_____

_____

_____

_____   *(4 marks)*

5 How is the poem made to seem positive in the final 8 lines?

_____

_____

_____

_____

_____

_____

_____

_____

_____

_____

_____

_____   *(8 marks)*

from Unrelated Incidents
by Tom Leonard

Might we have to translate this poem into standard English?

No. You need to understand what the poet is saying but it will be presumed you know
what it all means. Any question is likely to be about his attitude or what he believes in;
and about how he expresses himself and how the poem is structured.

1 What does the speaker think about BBC news presenters?

_____

_____

_____

_____

_____

_____
(3 marks)

2 What does the speaker think about people's attitudes to those with regional accents?

_____

_____

_____

_____

_____

_____

_____
(4 marks)

3 In your own words, sum up what he is saying about *'trooth'*.

_____

_____

_____

_____

_____

_____

_____
(4 marks)

4 In what ways is this a poem from a different culture?

_____

_____

_____

_____

_____

_____

_____

_____

_____ *(5 marks)*

5 How is the poem structured, and why?
Include comments on:

- how it is set out on the page
- the beginning and ending.

_____

_____

_____

_____

_____

_____

_____

_____

_____

_____ *(6 marks)*

6 What point is the poet trying to make by using such unusual spelling and such limited punctuation? Quote from the poem to support your opinions.

_____

_____

_____

_____

_____

_____

_____

_____

_____

_____ *(6 marks)*

Half-Caste
by John Agard

How serious is John Agard in this poem?

You can assume he is making a very serious point, but you might have to write about how he puts across his opinion. The other priorities are how the poem uses language and how it is structured.

1 What is the poet's message in this poem?

_____

_____

_____

_____

_____

_____ *(4 marks)*

2 Why has the poem been written in this style? Explain in detail.

_____

_____

_____

_____

_____

_____

_____

_____

_____ *(4 marks)*

3 Why is there so much repetition in the poem?

_____

_____

_____

_____

_____ *(4 marks)*

4 How is the idea of being *'half'* of something used by the poet?

_____

_____

_____

_____

_____

_____

_____

_____

_____

_____ *(6 marks)*

5 There are no full-stops in the poem. How has it been punctuated, and why?

_____

_____

_____

_____

_____

_____

_____ *(4 marks)*

6 What is the effect of the final 7 lines?

_____

_____

_____

_____

_____

_____

_____

_____

_____

_____ *(5 marks)*

Love After Love
by Derek Walcott

Since there does not seem to be a different culture in the poem, how do we handle it?

The poems in the selection are from different cultures and traditions, but are not necessarily about them. In this case, Walcott's poem offers a universal message which is not tied to a particular setting.

1 Why is the poem called 'Love After Love'?

_____

_____

_____

_____

_____

_____

_____

(4 marks)

2 How does the poet speak to the reader?

_____

_____

_____

_____

_____

_____

_____

_____

(4 marks)

3 What is the effect of the short sentences?

_____

_____

_____

_____

_____

(3 marks)

4 How does the poet create a sense of place?

_____

_____

_____

_____

_____

_____

_____

_____ *(4 marks)*

5 What is the mood of the poem? Comment on how it is created by:

- the opening
- the ending
- the poet's use of language.

_____

_____

_____

_____

_____

_____

_____

_____

_____

_____

_____

_____

_____

_____

_____

_____

_____

_____

_____

_____

_____ *(12 marks)*

This room
by Imtiaz Dharker

Is this another poem with no clear sense of location?

Imtiaz Dharker comes from India, but the poem could be set anywhere. The most important elements are what the poem has to say about an emotional time and how it says it.

1 What picture is created in *'This room'*?

_____

_____

_____

_____

_____

_____ *(4 marks)*

2 How is an atmosphere established in the first two stanzas?

_____

_____

_____

_____

_____

_____

_____

_____

_____

_____

_____ *(6 marks)*

3 Read lines 10 – 17 and explain how the poet has used:

• metaphor – when something is not literally true

• onomatopoeia – when words create sound

• enjambement – when there is no punctuation at the end of a line.

_____

_____

_____

_____

_____

_____

_____

_____

_____

_____

_____ *(6 marks)*

4 How is a sense of *'excitement'* sustained by the poet throughout the poem?
Explain:

- what happens
- how language is used.

_____

_____

_____

_____

_____

_____

_____

_____

_____

_____

_____

_____

_____

_____

_____ *(10 marks)*

5 The poem ends: *'my hands are outside, clapping'*. What is the effect of this line, and what
is the final impression presented to the reader?

_____

_____

_____

_____

_____ *(4 marks)*

Not my Business
by Niyi Osundare

Will we need to focus on each separate incident in the poem?

In some ways this is an 'easier' poem because it breaks into clear sections and the 'different culture' is obvious. However, you will need to be aware of the particular details, and the overall message we take from what happens. Of course, as ever, the poet's methods are important.

1 What happens to the people in the poem?

_____

_____

_____

_____

_____

_____

_____

_____

_____ *(4 marks)*

2 How has the poem been structured?

_____

_____

_____

_____

_____

_____

_____

_____

_____ *(4 marks)*

3 How does the speaker react at each stage in the poem and how does he feel at the end?

_____

_____

_____

_____

_____

_____

_____

_____

_____

_____

_____ *(4 marks)*

4 Why is the refrain *'What business of mine is it ..?'* repeated?

_____

_____

_____

_____ *(2 marks)*

5 How are we expected to react to the following lines?

- *Beat him soft like clay*
  And stuffed him down the belly
  Of a waiting jeep
- *Booted the whole house awake*
- *No query, no warning, no probe*
- *The jeep was waiting on my bewildered lawn*
  Waiting, waiting in its usual silence

_____

_____

_____

_____

_____

_____

_____

_____

_____

_____

_____

_____

_____

_____ *(7 marks)*

Presents from my Aunts in Pakistan by Moniza Alvi

This is the longest poem in the selection: should it be avoided?

You should be prepared to answer on any of the poems you have studied. There are so many things to say about culture in this poem that it certainly deserves close study.

1 What is the girl's problem? Explain in detail.

(4 marks)

2 What does she feel about her Pakistani culture?

(6 marks)

3 To what extent does she feel British?

(4 marks)

4 How is her Pakistani culture brought to life in the poem?
Comment on:

- the details
- the language used.

_____

_____

_____

_____

_____

_____

_____

_____

_____

_____

_____

_____

_____

_____

_____

_____

_____

_____

_____

_____

_____

_____ *(10 marks)*

5 Why is the ending important in our understanding of the girl's feelings?

_____

_____

_____

_____

_____ *(4 marks)*

Hurricane Hits England
by Grace Nichols

How can this be from a different culture, if it is set in England?

Like some other poems in the selection, this poem is about someone who is having to come to terms with a new culture. The culture of her original country is very different from the one in which she now finds herself. The poem is about her state of mind.

1 What has happened to make the poet consider her situation and what are her reactions?

_____
_____
_____
_____
_____
_____
_____
_____
_____
_____

(6 marks)

2 How are her emotions revealed to the reader? Refer closely to the text in your answer.

_____
_____
_____
_____
_____
_____
_____
_____
_____
_____
_____
_____
_____
_____
_____

(8 marks)

3 What connection does she find between the two cultures?

(4 marks)

4 How does she feel at the end? Explain.

(4 marks)

5 What do we learn about her original culture?
Consider:
- the details she includes
- the language used.

(10 marks)

Comparing poems

Are there any rules about which poems we compare? Do they have to be from the same cluster?

There will be two questions, from which you choose one. Which ever question you choose, you will always have to compare two poems. One poem is always named but the one you select can be from either cluster. Just be careful not to use one of the poems that are studied for Literature!

CLUSTER 1

Question: Compare *Night of the Scorpion* with any other poem of your choice. How do the poets present relationships in the poems?

1 Write your opening paragraph.

_____

_____

_____

_____

_____

_____

(3 marks)

2 Find points of comparison in the poems. Try to compare the ideas and the techniques.

Point of comparison	Reference: *Night of the Scorpion*	Reference: chosen poem	Comment/explanation

(12 marks)

3 Write your concluding paragraph.

_____

_____

_____

_____

_____

(3 marks)

4 You have already written an opening and ending. Now write the central section, the remainder of your response.

_____

_____

_____

_____

_____

_____

_____

_____

_____

_____

_____

_____

_____

_____

_____

_____

_____

_____

_____

_____

_____

_____

_____

_____

_____

_____

_____

_____

_____

_____

_____   _(21 marks)_

Continue on lined paper if necessary. Only spend 30 minutes on this task.

CLUSTER 2

Question: How is language used to reveal the speaker's situation in *Not My Business* and in any other poem of your choice?

1 What is the speaker's situation in *Not My Business*?

_____

_____

_____

_____

_____ *(3 marks)*

2 Which language might you comment on in *Not My Business*?

Quotation	Comment

Continue on lined paper if necessary.　　*(6 marks)*

3 What is the speaker's situation in your chosen poem?

_____

_____

_____

_____

_____ *(3 marks)*

4 What language might you comment on in your chosen poem?

Quotation	Comment

(6 marks)

5 Write the whole response, comparing the situations and the use of language.

_____

_____

_____

_____

_____

_____

_____

_____

_____

_____

_____

_____

_____

_____

_____

_____

_____

_____

_____

_____

_____

_____

_____

_____

_____

_____

_____

_____

_____

_____

_____

_____

_____

_____ _(27 marks)_

Continue on lined paper if necessary.

Paper 1 and 2 Section B: Types of writing and Writing skills

How to respond to the questions in Section B of both papers

While Section A on both papers tests your Reading ability, Section B assesses how successful you are at Writing. You will have 45 minutes to produce your response.

Section B of Paper 1 requires you to write to:

- argue
- persuade
- advise

or

- produce a mixture of these styles of writing.

Section B of Paper 2 requires you to write to:

- inform
- explain
- describe

or

- produce a mixture of these styles of writing.

Ideally, your response will be about 1½–2½ sides long. Remember that you will be assessed on the quality of your writing, not on how many sides of paper you can cover. It is better to write slightly less and to do it well.

You are likely to have to write a letter, an article, a speech, an advice sheet or a more traditional essay. Whatever the task, the basic requirements and the mark scheme will be the same.

You will be given two marks by the examiner:

1 for organisation and communication – 18 marks

2 for accuracy – 9 marks.

If you do well on one particular set of skills, it can compensate for a lower mark elsewhere.

You will be offered four questions and you must choose just one to answer. You only have three-quarters of an hour to write your response so it is essential that you choose the question that you feel is best for you and stick with it. There is not enough time to begin one essay then decide it might have been better to do another and change at that point.

The exam paper advises you on the basic approach that is best:

- plan your response
- write (aim for about 2 sides)
- check and improve your work.

Planning

The planning stage should take you 5 – 10 minutes. Aim to produce a detailed plan because if you include a good deal of detail it makes it easier for you to write a better essay. You can then concentrate on paragraphing, punctuation, vocabulary and expression because you have already decided what to write.

You might like to consider sequencing the ideas in your plan so that you have a 'route map'. You will then know where you are starting, what sections you will move through, and where you will finish:

Paragraph 1:

Paragraph 2:

… and so on.

Writing

The mark you are given for organisation and communication will be based on:

- how well you address the purpose and audience
- how interesting it is
- the quality of paragraphing
- the choice of vocabulary.

Your accuracy mark will be for:

- sentences
- spelling
- punctuation.

Checking

You should spend five minutes reading through your work, correcting and improving it. Try to read it slowly, focusing on each word. There are no marks for neatness, so change anything which is not as good as it should be but ensure that it is still readable!

Planning

Do we need to plan our written responses?

You are advised to plan your writing. Plotting your essay's development makes it develop more logically. Without planning, ideas tend to come in a random order and paragraphing can also be less effective.

Write a newspaper article in which you argue **either** for **or** against the idea that exams should be done away with and grades should be awarded for coursework alone.

1 Collect your ideas.

_____

_____

_____

_____

_____

_____

_____

_____   *(5 marks)*

2 Produce a detailed essay plan.

_____

_____

_____

_____

_____

_____

_____

_____

_____

_____

_____

_____

_____

_____

_____

_____

_____   *(10 marks)*

Continue on lined paper if necessary.

Describe a park in summer.

3 Collect your ideas.

_____

_____

_____

_____

_____

_____

_____

_____   _(5 marks)_

4 Produce a detailed essay plan.

_____

_____

_____

_____

_____

_____

_____

_____

_____

_____

_____

_____

_____

_____

_____

_____

_____

_____

_____

_____

_____

_____   _(10 marks)_

Continue on lined paper if necessary.

High quality features

What are 'high quality features'?

When the examiner reads through your Section B response, there are certain things which grab his attention. These make the writing more interesting and, as a result, you are more likely to be rewarded with higher marks. These features are included in the mark scheme used by the examiner.

Rhetorical questions

Rhetorical questions challenge the reader, to involve them in the ideas: e.g. 'Can this be right?'; 'Is there no other way to ..?'

1 Write the opening paragraph of an article for a national newspaper, to persuade readers that young people should be give the vote at the age of 16. Begin with rhetorical questions.

_____

_____

_____

_____

_____

_____

_____

_____

(6 marks)

Quotations

Quotations help to convince a reader, because they come from a different source. Usually, the quotation is from a person whose views might carry some weight (possibly the Prime Minister, a teacher, or a grandparent, depending on the topic).

2 Write the ending of a speech, in which you argue that the government should spend **either** more **or** less money on the armed forces.
Include at least one quotation.

_____

_____

_____

_____

_____

_____

_____

_____

_____

_____

(6 marks)

Examples, facts and figures and anecdotes

You can make what you are saying more convincing by using examples, facts and figures and anecdotes (brief stories, to illustrate a point). Because you do not have access to research materials in the exam, you will have to call on personal knowledge; or you might wish to invent details to support your views.

3 In a letter, you are informing a pen friend about what your school is like. Write a paragraph in which you include some relevant examples.

_____

_____

_____

_____

_____

_____

_____

_____

_____

_____   *(6 marks)*

4 Write a further paragraph, in which you include some facts and figures about exam performances in your school.

_____

_____

_____

_____

_____

_____

_____

_____   *(6 marks)*

5 Write a final paragraph, which includes an anecdote that shows what life is like for you at school.

_____

_____

_____

_____

_____

_____

_____   *(6 marks)*

Similes and metaphors

Similes and metaphors make your writing more interesting. They help the reader interpret your ideas. Similes make a comparison, using 'like' or 'as'. Metaphors say something which is not literally true

6 Complete this description of your best friend.

Whenever I need help, she/he is like _____

Of course, at other times, she/he can be as _____

as _____

In general, though, she/he (use a metaphor here) _____

_____ *(3 marks)*

7 Explain why you particularly enjoy a hobby or pastime. Try to include at least three or four similes or metaphors in your answer.

_____

_____

_____

_____

_____

_____

_____

_____

_____

_____ *(6 marks)*

Emotive language

Emotive language touches the emotions, perhaps making us feel sympathy, happiness, or whatever: e.g. 'Try to imagine what it is like to be without food and water for days at a time …'

8 Write a paragraph in which you advise a relative to give some of their money to a charity of your choice. Use some emotive language.

_____

_____

_____

_____

_____

_____

_____

_____

_____

_____

_____ *(6 marks)*

Humour

Humour should be used carefully: too much humour might not be the best approach. However, if you can make the examiner smile, that is rarely a bad thing. For example, you might wish to poke fun at someone or something, and exaggeration is often a useful tool.

9 Complete this paragraph which describes school meals, continuing the sarcasm.

The meals themselves would not have been out of place in a Siberian camp for mass murderers, train spotters or maths teachers. The mashed potato _____

_____

However, that was positively delicious, compared to the gravy: _____

_____

As for the meat and vegetables – well, they _____

Then, there was the pudding! _____ *(4 marks)*

10 Write part of a sales sheet, to persuade people to buy your house. Make the house seem attractive, but try to end with a humorous remark.

_____

_____

_____

_____

_____

_____

_____ *(6 marks)*

The unfinished sentence

Using an ellipsis (…) shows that the sentence has not been completed, and allows the reader to imagine what might have come next. This too can produce a smile: 'And as for the contents of his pockets …'

11 As the ending to an argumentative piece of writing about why we should **or** should not eat more healthily, finish with an ellipsis.

_____

_____

_____

_____

_____

_____

_____

_____ *(6 marks)*

Paragraphing

Paragraphing is a significant part of the Writing mark scheme. If you can vary your paragraph lengths effectively, you will receive a higher grade.

12 Write a section of a response which advises young people to choose their friends carefully. Try to write:

- a paragraph of about 8 – 10 lines which explains why it is wise to choose friends carefully
- a longer, descriptive paragraph, to describe the kinds of 'bad friends' you can attract
- a short, punchy paragraph to make your feelings about such people very clear.

(18 marks)

Continue on lined paper if necessary.

Punctuation

You will impress the examiner if you include a variety of punctuation (e.g. full-stops, capitals, commas, exclamation marks, question marks, quotation marks, colons and semi-colons …)

13 Re-write this paragraph, introducing more varied punctuation. Try to stay as faithful to the original as possible, concentrating on altering the punctuation, rather than the words.

The desert is cold at night. All the animals and insects seem to come to life. Overhead the moon beams down. Anyone lost and wondering feels like crying. What can I do? Where can I go for rest and safety? Such are their cries. Yet the desert is merciless and does not give any sign of hope or rescue. There is piercing cold. There is howling wind and shifting sand. There is just hopelessness.

_____

_____

_____

_____

_____

_____

_____

_____ *(5 marks)*

14 Write the opening paragraph(s) of a response in which you inform readers of a magazine for teenagers about how to prepare a quick meal for their friends. Make the punctuation as varied as possible.

_____

_____

_____

_____

_____

_____

_____

_____

_____

_____

_____

_____

_____

_____ *(8 marks)*

Opening and concluding paragraphs

Are the start and the ending particularly important?

There are no specific marks for those paragraphs, but you are likely to benefit if you impress the examiner with your beginning; and the final paragraph is the last thing he reads before putting a mark on your work.

Write a letter to advise your cousin about what to do with the rest of his/her life, since he/she is about to leave school.

1 Write the opening paragraph. Remember that high quality features will make your writing more distinctive.

_____

_____

_____

_____

_____

_____

_____

_____

_____ *(6 marks)*

2 Write the final paragraph.
Try to make it:

- memorable
- link with an idea or ideas in your opening.

_____

_____

_____

_____

_____

_____

_____

_____ *(6 marks)*

Write a section for a school brochure, to explain to new students how to avoid problems with teachers at school.

3 Write the opening paragraph, making it serious in tone.

_____

_____

_____

_____

_____

_____

_____ *(6 marks)*

4 Write an alternative opening, which is more light-hearted.

_____

_____

_____

_____

_____

_____

_____ *(6 marks)*

5 Write the concluding paragraph to either of the openings you have produced.

_____

_____

_____

_____

_____

_____

_____

_____

_____ *(6 marks)*

Writing to argue

What is the most important thing to remember when writing to argue?

It is vital that an argument includes alternative viewpoints. These do not have to be balanced, but there can be no argument unless there is something to argue against.

Argue that more help should **or** should not be given to people who regularly break the law.

1 Make a list of points for and against the idea that more help should be given.

For	Against

(6 marks)

2 Read this opening paragraph. Totally re-write the paragraph, maintaining the point of view but including:

- an appropriate topic sentence
- more variety in the language and sentences
- at least one high quality feature.

> My family has had lots of trouble with people who break the law. We shouldn't help them. I think a lot of the punishments are great. Some people want to be nice to criminals. I think they are mad. One man in the paper spent nearly all his life in prison. He kept breaking the law. He needed to be punished.

_____

_____

_____

_____

_____

_____

_____

_____

(6 marks)

3 Write a paragraph in which you balance two opposing points of view about how criminals should be treated, but end the paragraph by supporting one of the viewpoints.

_____

_____

_____

_____

_____

_____ *(6 marks)*

4 Write a paragraph supporting your own opinion, in which you use a convincing example, anecdote, quotation and/or statistic(s).

_____

_____

_____

_____

_____

_____ *(6 marks)*

5 Write a paragraph which follows from the one you have just written. Make sure you:

- link them effectively
- offer an opposing viewpoint
- end the paragraph by returning to your original opinion.

_____

_____

_____

_____

_____

_____

_____

_____

_____ *(6 marks)*

Practice essay title

Write an article for your local newspaper, arguing that there is too much pressure upon teenagers and that they should be allowed to enjoy 'the best years of their lives'.

Writing to persuade

What is the difference between writing to argue and writing to persuade?

Sometimes, we persuade by arguing effectively. It is also possible to persuade by presenting just one point of view and often a range of techniques is used, such as emotive language, convincing examples and appropriate anecdotes.

Write a letter to the Prime Minister to persuade him to give a large sum of money so that part of your school can be rebuilt.

1 List at least five convincing reasons why you need the money.

_____

_____

_____

_____

_____ *(5 marks)*

2 Write a paragraph explaining one of the reasons, using an anecdote (something that has happened) to illustrate your point.

_____

_____

_____

_____

_____

_____

_____

_____

_____

_____ *(6 marks)*

3 Write another paragraph, about a different point, this time including emotive language to convince the Prime Minister. (Emotive language touches the emotions.)

_____

_____

_____

_____

_____

_____

_____

_____

_____ *(6 marks)*

4 Write another paragraph. In this case, include humour or exaggeration.

_____
_____
_____
_____
_____
_____
_____
_____   *(6 marks)*

5 Write your concluding paragraph. Sum up your reasons for asking for the money and try to make an effective final plea.

_____
_____
_____
_____
_____
_____
_____
_____
_____   *(6 marks)*

Practice essay title

Either:
Writing as a celebrity chef, produce a newspaper column to persuade parents to encourage their children to eat healthily.

Or:
Writing as a famous sports personality, produce a newspaper column to persuade parents to encourage their children to lead a healthier lifestyle.

Writing to advise

What is the key to effective advice?

Advice needs to appeal to the reader's sense of logic in order to be accepted. Careful planning is essential if the reader is to be convinced. The ideas can be supported by evidence or anecdote, as well as emotive touches, rhetoric and so on.

As an agony aunt who offers advice to readers in a daily newspaper, give advice to a mother who has written to you because her teenage son or daughter seems to be out of control.

1 Produce a list of problems with the teenager; and brief notes about what your advice will be to remedy the problem.

Problem	Advice

(5 marks)

Advice is sometimes placed together, after the problem or problems have been outlined. In this case, though, offer the advice in stages:

2 Select one of the problems and write a paragraph which explains what the problem is and how to remedy it.

Use a brief anecdote to support your solution.

_____

_____

_____

_____

_____

_____

_____

_____

_____

_____

(6 marks)

3 Deal with another problem. This time, use evidence and emotive language to convince the audience.

_____

_____

_____

_____

_____

_____

_____   *(6 marks)*

4 Select another problem, but this time use humour in your response to it.

_____

_____

_____

_____

_____

_____

_____

_____   *(6 marks)*

5 Write your concluding paragraph. Remember to finish with an approach designed to make the reader follow your advice.

_____

_____

_____

_____

_____

_____

_____   *(6 marks)*

Practice essay title

Write an article for your local newspaper, to advise residents how to protect their homes against burglars.

Combining skills on Paper 1 Section B

How do we write in different styles?

It is not really a question of writing in totally different styles. After all, arguing, persuading and advising are sometimes very closely linked. However, an option on Section B will be to write a response which involves more than one kind of writing. You might be asked to argue and persuade or you might be faced with another combination.

Write an article for a local newspaper in which you **persuade** readers to help with charity fundraising. **Argue** that the cause you are supporting is one of the best, and **advise** readers about how they can get involved.

1 Plan your article in detail, making sure that you will be persuading, arguing and advising.

(6 marks)

2 Write a persuasive first paragraph, in which you include a quotation and some statistics. You can invent the material, but make sure it sounds convincing.

_____

_____

_____ *(6 marks)*

3 Write two other paragraphs which:

- are well linked
- are designed to argue, persuade and advise
- use a range of appropriate techniques.

_____

_____

_____

_____

_____

_____

_____

_____

_____

_____

_____

_____

_____

_____

_____

_____ *(12 marks)*

4 Write your conclusion, making it effective.

_____

_____

_____

_____

_____

_____

_____ *(6 marks)*

Practice essay title

Write a letter to advise a relative about how to spend money they have inherited recently and persuade them to spend some of it on other members of the family.

Writing to inform

Isn't it easy to simply present information?

It can be relatively straightforward, but the examiner will still be looking for a wide range of skills: structure, paragraphing, accuracy and high quality features, as well as variety in the language itself. In addition, the response must be appropriate for the purpose and audience.

Write a section for a guide book for visitors to this country, to inform them about what Britain has to offer.

1 Write a list of significant features or areas of interest that you intend to discuss in detail. Aim to include a range of ideas.

_____

_____

_____

_____

_____

_____ *(3 marks)*

2 Write the opening paragraph. Aim to interest the reader.

_____

_____

_____

_____

_____

_____

_____

_____

_____ *(6 marks)*

3 Write the next paragraph, including relevant facts or statistics and a related quotation. Facts, statistics and quotations can be invented, so long as they sound convincing.

_____

_____

_____

_____

_____

_____

_____

_____

_____

_____   *(6 marks)*

4 Write the final two paragraphs, including a touch of humour if possible. Remember you
need to:

- appeal to your target audience
- interest the reader
- round off your response effectively.

_____

_____

_____

_____

_____

_____

_____

_____

_____

_____

_____

_____

_____

_____

_____

_____   *(12 marks)*

Practice essay title

There has been some bad publicity in the press about the area in which you live. Write a
letter to your local Member of Parliament, to inform him or her about the good things that
happen in your area.

Writing to explain

When you write to inform, you give facts and opinions about the subject of your essay. When you explain, you are saying why something happens, or how a situation arises. You move beyond the obvious, to give reasons for things.

Explain how to stay healthy.

1 Produce a spider diagram of ideas.

(6 marks)

Now, structure them into a logical sequence.

Main ideas for staying healthy e.g. cycle regularly	Explanation of 'how' e.g. buy new bike, find necessary time …
1	
2	
3	
4	
5	
6	

2 Write about your first idea, saying why it is the most important.

_____

_____

_____

_____

_____

_____

_____

_____

_____

_____   *(6 marks)*

3 Write another paragraph of your choice, including facts and figures (which you can invent) and an emotive appeal (touching the reader's emotions) about why this way of staying healthy is so important.

_____

_____

_____

_____

_____

_____

_____

_____

_____

_____   *(6 marks)*

4 Conclude your essay, summarising your ideas.

_____

_____

_____

_____

_____

_____

_____   *(6 marks)*

Practice essay title

Write an essay for a magazine for teenagers, in which you explain how teenagers can be fashionable. You might wish to write about clothes, music or lifestyles.

Writing to describe

What sort of description will be required?

It is unlikely you will be expected to produce a story. The question will probably ask you to describe a person or place. If that is the case, avoid the temptation to write a narrative.

Describe the most unusual person you have ever met.

1 Write an introductory paragraph, in which you describe the person in general terms and make clear why he/she is unusual.

_____

_____

_____

_____

_____

_____

_____

_____ *(6 marks)*

2 List three similes and three metaphors which you can use in your description.

Similes

- _____

- _____

- _____

Metaphors

- _____

- _____

- _____ *(6 marks)*

3 Extend your description, by writing further paragraphs which use your similes and metaphors and give an indication of what the person looks like and how he or she behaves. You might also wish to include incidents in which the person has been involved, speech, others' opinions of the person, and so on. If necessary, continue on lined paper.

_____

_____

_____

_____

_____

_____

_____

_____

_____

_____

_____

_____

_____

_____

_____

_____

_____

_____

_____

_____

_____

_____

_____

_____

_____

(15 marks)

4 Write a concluding paragraph, to sum up your feelings about this person.

_____

_____

_____

_____

_____

_____

(6 marks)

Practice essay title

Describe a scene in winter.

Combining skills on Paper 2 Section B

It is exactly the same situation. One of the essay titles offered will ask to inform and explain, to explain and describe, and so on.

Some students are arriving from another country, on an exchange trip.
Write a handout sheet to inform them about things they need to know about this country; and to explain the most important laws.

1 Things they need to know about this country

_____
_____
_____
_____
_____

Important laws

_____
_____
_____
_____
_____   *(6 marks)*

2 Write a brief and welcoming first paragraph.

_____
_____
_____
_____
_____
_____
_____   *(4 marks)*

3 Write three paragraphs which give information and explanation. Remember to:
- be precise and detailed in your information
- explain how the laws work and why they are necessary.

_____

_____

_____

_____

_____

_____

_____

_____

_____

_____

_____

_____

_____

_____

_____

_____

_____

_____

_____   _(12 marks)_

Continue on lined paper if necessary.

4 Conclude your sheet in a way that is appropriate for the purpose and audience.

_____

_____

_____

_____

_____

_____

_____   _(6 marks)_

Practice essay title

Describe your favourite television programme and explain why you enjoy it.

Revision advice

Working through the sections in this book will have helped you to focus on the important elements in each part of the exam.

You can extend your revision and preparation in various ways.

Section A Paper 1

Try to spend five minutes each day examining a text. For example, if you have a newspaper, decide how the writers have set out to influence their purposes and audiences.

You might adopt this sort of routine:

Day 1: how presentational devices have been used in a text

Day 2: how an argument has been constructed

Day 3: how facts and opinions have been used in an article

Day 4: how language has been used in a report

Day 5: how successful a particular writer has been and why

and so on.

Section A Paper 2

It is relatively easy to read through all the poems from different cultures and traditions, but that is not necessarily the best way to prepare for your exam.

Instead, try working on one poem each day. Read a poem and make sure you know:

• exactly what the poet is saying (ideas, feelings, attitudes)

• how the poet says it (language and structure).

Choose a different poem the next day, and make the same decisions. In addition, decide in what ways it is the same as the other poem, or different. Deal with the other poems in the same way.

Section B responses

The more you practise the vital skills, the better you are likely to perform in the exam.

Consider:

• setting your own titles and producing detailed plans

• writing sections of the essays, which include high quality features

• producing responses in 45 minutes

• checking your work for errors and making appropriate improvements.

Remember to check your answers for free online: **www.collinseducation.com/revision**

Reading media and non-fiction answers

Most of the answers that follow are not 'the correct answers' but should help you to see the sort of answer you would need to write in order to get a Grade C. As a reminder, here is an outline of the skills you need to show at different grades at GCSE:

Grade	Skills demonstrated
F/G	• some simple supported comment • mainly narrative content – re-telling what is in the article • some appropriate detail • some reference to the question
D/E	• some extended comment, supported • unstructured response – tends to re-tell in own words • some identification of main points • attempts to answer question
B/C	• clear attempt to answer question • organised response • selects details and comments on them • a variety of information and comment

Pages 102–103

1

The writer wants to tell us about Michael Pelham and what he has done. He makes Michael seem like a hero: 'Hero beats the Atlantic'. He explains how Michael survived on his own for six weeks on the sea and managed to cope with all sorts of problems, like larger ships and even sharks. However, he says that Michael has even bigger problems to come because his GCSEs are next – especially since he will now find himself behind in all his subjects. The writer might want us to feel sorry for Michael, or expect us to think that he will be able manage with no problems, because Michael can cope with everything...

2

Extract	Audience	Reason for decision
'For the woman in your life: "Erotique", the new fragrance by Henri.'	Probably men *(1 mark)*	Any suitable comment on 'For the woman in your life' *(1 mark)* **Or** any comment on 'Erotique', suggesting romantic involvement *(1 mark)*
'Throughout the nineteenth century, nurses continued to do as they were told by doctors. They knew their place.'	Those learning about history, or the history of medicine *(1 mark)* **Or** general readership interested in medical/ historical matters *(1 mark)*	Appropriate comment on historical nature of material *(1 mark)* Appropriate reference to 'doctors' and 'nurses' *(1 mark)*
'Discipline your children. No longer can they be allowed to do exactly as they wish.'	Parents *(1 mark)* Looking for or needing advice *(1 mark)*	'Your children' *(1 mark)* (Strict) tone: 'discipline', 'No longer can they...' *(1 mark)*
'Investors in Sun Life Assurance of Canada rejoiced earlier today, as share values reached unprecedented heights.'	Possibly readers of business news *(1 mark)* **Or** newspaper readers *(1 mark)* **Or** investors *(1 mark)* **Or** relatively educated audience *(1 mark)*	Subject matter deals with finance ('share values') *(1 mark)* Apparently newsworthy content ('Investors... rejoiced earlier today...') *(1 mark)* Relatively complex language ('unprecedented heights') *(1 mark)*

The advertisement is for those who want to visit Paris. It aims to attract them by making it seem exciting ('wonderful') and uses a lot of language that might make visitors want to go with Leger Holidays – they mention a free brochure and the fact that there is Silver Service luxury. It all seems very 'easy'…

Pages 104–105

1 Any <u>five</u> from:

- top rock band played
- played free for nearly 2 hours
- Jodie – and everyone she knew – was invited
- it was a dream come true
- manager chatted to Jodie
- she received gifts from band

2 'The manager chatted to Jodie for an hour': the group did not!

3 Any <u>four</u> from:

- shot for desertion
- name not on Shoreham war memorial
- fought at Mons and Le Cateau at age of 19
- he 'cracked'
- and ran away

The man who is writing knows all about Private Jack Brown. He knows about him being shot but also makes it seem that Jack had good reason for running away because the battles seemed really bad. He has sympathy for the young boy. He says that he was just like Jack: 'I was on active service at the age of 18', but he didn't have such a bad time: 'I didn't undergo 1 pc of this lad's experience'. He says that anyone would be afraid if they were being fired on. So he wants Shoreham to put Jack's name on the memorial…

Pages 106–107

The writer thinks that British holidaymakers just behave badly when they are abroad. They don't go for what is there, they just carry on as if they were at home:

'It's about bringing Britain with you.'

She writes about what the holidaymakers are like and they do not sound attractive. They eat and drink too much, for example. She is worried because they are racist and do not like where they are so they stay by the pool and enjoy their smoking and their crosswords but they do not mix with the other cultures…

The writer thinks there are two sides to Jaggers' personality. He could be a violent man, because he killed his 15 year old cousin. The movie director said Jaggers was 'evil'. It sounds like he was a big gangster in London. Miranda Standbridge, though, was fond of him. She talked about his charity work and said he was kind. This might have been because he attended church regularly and he was also good to his mother: 'a loving son to his mother'…

The writer does not seem too sure whether Jaggers was a good man or not. We can tell this because he points out lots of things that Jaggers did wrong but also says some of the good things he did too. For instance, he picks out that Jaggers went to church and that he appeared at many charity events, even if we do not know how much money he actually gave himself. His mother loved him too. But the writer also knows he did bad things like killing his cousin and because this comes at the end it might be what he wants us to remember…

Pages 108–109

1 Facts and opinions include:

Facts	Opinions
checking temperatures etc	white expanse is 'incredible' and provides 'delights'
has had more spare time	whales were 'Fantastic'
has been on a boat and seen whales	penguins are 'crazy'/'not very bright'
has seen seals and skuas	penguins 'panic'
has seen penguins	birds are 'stupid'
was in boat when penguin dropped in	'maybe he thought we were a taxi'
collected glacier ice	'best thing yet' is the ice
kept ice in fridge then put it in drinks	'It's not like normal blue glacier ice'

The writer seems to be having a wonderful time in the Antarctic. She gives facts about what she has done, and they all seem like fun: 'I've been out on a boat… Orca whales swam past…'. The facts give a picture of her life. We know about her job, checking the temperatures and so on and what happens, like the penguin jumping in the boat and how she gets the chance to drink old ice. However, she uses opinions too. She makes us think that the penguins are crazy and describes them as 'stupid'. It is her opinion that the penguin thought the boat was a taxi, but maybe it was just confused. Overall, though, we agree with her opinions that the Antarctic is 'incredible' and 'fantastic'…

The reader is told many positive facts about Jennifer Aniston, like how much she was paid for 'Friends' and about the Emmy prizes and being on the cover of Vanity Fair. She has also been in movies and had 'rave reviews'. All these things make us think she is good. The writer's opinion is that she has nothing to worry about in the world, because he describes her as 'beautiful' and 'talented'. He also thinks that she is so wonderful 'she won't be single for long'. He even gives his positive opinion of her hair…

Pages 110–111

1 Main points in the argument:

- Many educated people read little but will not admit it:
- 'refuse to admit they read so little'
- They pretend because they do not want to be 'shown up':
- 'Life is too competitive, even when you leave the playground'
- Even those who do read exaggerate:
- 'I was re-reading it recently and…'
- We should not think that only people who read are wise:
- 'They too have their wisdom'
- People who do not read can have many other talents which are just as valuable, though they can be overlooked:
- 'The world isn't logical'

Each point needs to be supported by a relevant quotation. Those given are merely examples.

The writer starts off with a question, to involve the reader. Whilst we are trying to work out an answer, he tells us why people lie about what they have been reading: 'Because they feel shown up'. He argues that we should not make up things we have read or even boast about what we have read, because people do other things that are interesting. He proves this point by mentioning Casualty and Coronation Street and Eastenders, which most people will think are just as interesting as books. At the end he also writes about the doctor, who thinks that people look down on him if he doesn't reads, but they don't know all the things he knows, which is not really fair. This is all to make us believe that the writer is right…

Pages 112–113

Other answers would be acceptable for these questions, as long as they make sense and are clearly explained.

- A conversational opening: 'Let's face it' – to attract a wide audience.
- Use of a cliché (metaphor): 'not always everyone's cup of tea' – for same purpose, not appearing too intellectual.

2
- Exaggeration for effect: 'left most of the audience…' – to criticise the show and make the disapproval seem unanimous
- Mention of Big Brother and Eastenders – once more, to appeal to a wide, everyday audience
- Mention of Shakespeare as 'the Bard' – showing the writer is educated
- Violent vocabulary to show how badly the play was produced: 'spat out, rushed and mutilated' – shows emotions of writer
- Play on words: 'obscene and best not heard' (changed from 'Children should be seen and not heard') – to add a touch of humour and, again, suggesting intelligence in the writer.

3
- Simple statement: 'Nothing was as it should be' – which seems indisputable.
- Contrast between traditional view ('Shakespeare's final great creation') and this version, made to seem cheap and sordid ('perverse and perverted')
- Characters seem mad and unpleasant: 'deranged' and 'hideously naked' – putting

further personal interpretation on the performance.

- Descriptions of characters make them seem like characters out of a mad house.

4 • Alliteration used: 'foul freaks' – frightening/unpleasant 'f' sounds.
- Simple statements again, making straightforward points which, it seems, cannot be contradicted.

5 Extract from a Grade C answer

The writer uses rhetorical questions to make the reader pay attention: 'Why aren't they like young people in Britain?' She tries to keep our attention by putting questions right to the end of the text, and by using imagery: 'It's like trying to cork a bottle of beer.' This makes it seem like the children are all out of control. The teachers are made to seem like jailers, with 'rods of iron', trying to keep order in schools. There are lots of lists when the children are out of school ('ball games, smokers, shrieks') to make it all seem really mad…

Pages 114–115

1 Extract from a Grade C answer

The writer starts out by asking why children in Britain behave so badly. She also says that they are not so bad abroad. This is the main idea, and it comes back again at the end, when the writer is asking the same question: 'Why does it happen here?'

Next, the writer says what goes wrong, starting with schools. The children seem to be out of control, like beer spilling over, and the teachers are like people guarding them, but once they get outside, everyone has to watch out. Then there is a third paragraph describing their behaviour once the children can do what they want when school is over. This is all building up, as if it goes from bad to worse…

2 Extract from a Grade C answer

The advertisement is not about anything exciting, but they have tried to organise it so that it catches our eye. First of all we notice 'Headteacher' and the numbers underneath, which might encourage someone to apply for the job. Above it, of course, is the name of the school, and people need to see

that so they will be encouraged to apply for somewhere next to the sea. The next thing that catches the eye is the grey box, and that has details in it of what the school is looking for. Again, it is not exciting, but they have tried to set it out on a slant, so it looks more impressive. The text underneath gives more details, but like an article, so the ending details stand out again, since they are in bold… You could say that the things in the advertisement are actually set out in order of real importance, beginning with the school, then the job, and so on…

3 Extract from a Grade C answer

The picture captures the reader's attention by showing a picture of the Beatles. They have all got earpieces in, as if they are listening to their ipods, because their music is set to be downloaded. Above the picture is the headline 'Beatlemania', which would tell anyone who the men are and sums up the article. That is why it comes first. The reason this is such a big story is put next: it is all going to make '£500m a year'. If anyone might be thinking this is not especially important, the text box is headed 'Exclusive', to keep the excitement going…

Pages 116–117

1 Extract from a Grade C answer

The text is setting out to attract the audience by making the idea of stopping the sun's heat both simple and interesting. The most obvious feature is the illustration. We see how huge mirrors could be put above the earth. This is just how the system would work. The headline 'How technology could help' gives the basic message and stands out at the top of the page. The actual article, though, is headed with 'Let's block sun with smoke and mirrors', which tells the reader exactly what will happen. Beside it, there is a cartoon, presumably to make the reader laugh, but it is hard to see what it is saying. Of course, if the reader wants to know exactly how the system will work, there are also captions, explaining the illustration…

2 Extract from a Grade C answer

The first thing you notice in the advert is the main character in the foreground. It is suggesting that the book, which is also shown, is going to be about dead people, or someone from a life after death, because he is a skeleton. Being dressed in ordinary clothes, though, it makes it look as if he is going to try to be a part of our world. The grin on his face makes him look quite happy, not too frightening, so maybe this will be a book for younger children. The font for the writing is also quite jokey...

3 Possible answers include:

Orange: impression of fun ... maybe reminding us of an orange drink ... a summery colour ... bright ('in your face') colour, to attract young readers ... making the book seem not too serious

Silver: cold and more frightening ... like steel ... or the coldness of stars ... clinical ... lifeless, in a way...

Pages 118–119

1 James Morrison: only drink mentioned is beer – and it's all very casual (£30 a bottle; Carling, Becks, Corona; beer has a bad effect on your throat or makes you gassy)

In contrast:

WaterAid website: water is a matter of life and death – and the problems caused by dirty water are listed

2 James Morrison

- Purpose: to entertain or inform
- Support will select appropriate detail about James Morrison's lifestyle
- Audience: likely to be casual reader or fan
- Support likely to focus on the 'lightweight' nature of the text – there is nothing of any real importance here

WaterAid:

- Purpose: to inform about the conditions and, perhaps, at the end, suggest that politicians should do more to help (It is never stated, but perhaps, because of the nature of the material, they are hoping to gain support for their cause)
- Support might identify the most serious diseases, significant detail or the final paragraph, as relevant
- Audience: web-surfers, those who are seeking information, supporters of WaterAid Support likely to mention it is from a website and/or precise details of diseases and close focus on the water situation

3 | **Extract from a Grade C answer**

The James Morrison piece does use facts to say what has happened to him, but there are also opinions to tell you how he feels about it all. Many of them are adjectives like 'amazing' and 'posh' and 'incredible'. It all sounds like the way he would say things. On the other hand, the WaterAid extract has much more important facts. It tells the reader all about diseases and how many children are killed by bad water every day. Its opinion is more formal, and tells us that this suffering is wrong: 'Access to water is a basic human need and ... right'...

Pages 122–123

Foundation Tier

1a Up to <u>six</u> of:

- more sensible to holiday in Britain: weather warming and less carbon dioxide released
- we have all seen what the rest of the world has to offer
- Mediterranean is polluted
- the world is now becoming much the same – McDonald's everywhere
- Spain and Greece no longer cheap places to stay
- there are many wonderful places to visit in Britain
- there is no problem getting to these places

1b Any two points, but they must have sensible reasons.

1c | **Extract from a Grade C answer**

The writer tries to make us agree with him by using facts like we use a lot of fuel flying and it would be better if we stayed at home. He says that millions of Britons fly and that is a fact, but he thinks Britain is just as good as abroad, and that is an opinion. All the time he keeps comparing Britain with places in other countries. He names lots of places that are good, in his opinion, places like Croyde and Morar...

... All the time he tries to sound convincing. The last paragraph shows that in his opinion we will have to stop flying but Wales is wonderful. He ends by quoting Hamlet, to make it sound as if he is intelligent enough to know important things.

The text is obviously for people who have enough money to go to places like the hotel being described. They would have to be rich enough to pay for it ('£190 per room per night') and would have to be able to cope with the food. It seems different from what most people might eat, because they give you things like 'oven-baked shrimps' and something else called 'grouper'. Most people won't even know what that is...

2 Extract from a Grade C answer

The texts are very different so they try to interest the readers in different ways. 'Need a break' has rhetorical questions in the title, to try to involve the reader in what is going on, so we read the rest. It talks about Bognor, so it is trying to make us laugh. On the other hand, 'Ancient art' sounds as if it is all from back in time because of the word 'ancient' and it is about holidays because of the word 'relaxing'. Obviously it is going to go on about how to have a good rest...

Higher Tier

1a Extract from a Grade A* answer

To understand the full argument, the reader would have to be reasonably intelligent. The text deals with details about potential disaster for the world, with foreign destinations and places in Britain: the audience, presumably, would already be aware of these things. In addition, the audience will be the sort of people who have the funds to travel widely, because this argument would be wasted on those earning low wages who cannot afford holidays to begin with. The text is intended to make the readers think about their behaviour and its possible repercussions – for the world itself, which is faced with a frightening future and even 'catastrophic water shortages'...

1b Extract from a Grade B answer

The writer offers a logical argument. She says that we must stay at home, otherwise the world will become over-polluted. However, that is no hardship, because Britain is as good as the continent and we can see everything we need to on television. It is also as cheap to stay where we are.

The text itself is full of facts and opinions. The facts are things like 5.5% of Britain's carbon dioxide coming from aircraft fuel. This is bound to make the reader think. She also offers opinions like 'Air travel is feeding our destruction'. It sounds like we are feeding an animal that will destroy us...

2a Extract from a Grade A answer

If you are advertising a hotel, it would be foolish not to include pictures. They are the most likely device to attract readers – and, potentially, visitors. In this case, the reader's eye is immediately attracted to the picture of the Acropolis. It is a sight known across the world. And in case the reader did not recognise it, the name is put in bold and in capitals beneath. It looks like one of the wonders of the world, and especially so when directly beside a heading like 'Ancient art of relaxing' – the 'ancient' nature of the place is stressed here and stands out. The caption beneath the picture links the view to the hotel and is again in bold, so as not to be missed...

2b Extract from a Grade A* answer

The writer of 'Need a break' begins with rhetorical questions; but if they do not challenge us enough, adds a touch of apparent sarcasm; 'Why not try Bognor..?' We are, presumably, expected to be amazed or chuckle, then read on. We are hooked.

In contrast, the writer then becomes much more formal and factual. The use of government figures and a statistic is meant to appeal to our logical and practical sensibilities; and the short, punchy sentence hammers home an immediate message: 'Air travel is feeding our destruction.' The metaphor is meant to be frightening...

Reading poetry answers

Answers to many poetry questions may be a very personal response, so there is rarely a right or wrong answer. The grid below shows you the sort of skills you need to show at each GCSE grade – what the examiner will be looking for when he or she marks your paper. The points that follow indicate the most likely points that answers to different questions would contain. Some questions also have an extract from a sample answer. Visit www.collinseducation.com/revision for more guidance.

Grade	Skills demonstrated
G	• simple comment • reference to some detail • able to say something simple about how the poet has written the poem
F	• some simple supported comment • reference to appropriate detail • simple statement on two or more aspects of presentation e.g. 'The poet uses a simile'
E	• some simple extended comment, joining ideas together • appropriate quotation to support points made • simple comments on aspects of presentation e.g. 'The simile makes us think that …'
D	• able to mention feelings or ideas or attitudes in the poems • range of supported comments • comments on how things in the poem affect the reader e.g. 'This makes us feel sad, as "…"'
C	• understanding of feelings or ideas or attitudes – clearly explained • range of extended supported comment • some detail of what the poet intended to do and how he achieved it
B	• able to explain the feelings or ideas or attitudes • effective use of textual detail: the right quotations used in effective ways • understanding of a variety of the poet's techniques and purposes – clearly supported from the poem
A	• exploration of and empathy with writer's feelings, attitudes and ideas: a range of interpretations • references integrated into response so it all flows effectively • analysis of how the writer achieved effects: in depth, looking at layers of meaning
A*	• consistent insight and convincing imaginative interpretation: candidate understands everything about the poet's intentions and how the effects are achieved • close textual analysis

Limbo

Pages 126–127

1 Answers are likely to include:

- Slaves being transported to America
- Slaves singing/dancing
- Slaves being treated harshly
- Desperation of slaves on the ocean
- Possibly interpretation of 'knees spread wide'
- Interpretation of the ending; salvation or further misery on solid ground

2 Answers are likely to include:

- Onomatopoeia – 'stick' and 'whip' and what the sounds suggest
- The repetition of the sound
- Alliteration – 'dark deck' and what the sounds suggest
- Metaphor – 'dark deck is slavery': what this suggests about slavery

3 Answers are likely to suggest:

- Song that the slaves are singing, and why
- It is repeated, maybe to suggest length of voyage and their suffering
- 'limbo' set under 'limbo', to show the way they go down
- Interpretations of 'limbo': such as the dance, the state between heaven and hell, as something that keeps them going, something they are made to do, showing how they are being forced down…

4 Answers are likely to cover ideas such as:

- To create the rhythm and sound of the dancing on the ship
- Italicised sections might have a different emphasis – maybe as they are chanted by all
- Explanations of line such as:
- 'long dark deck and the water surrounding me
- long dark deck and the silence is over me'
- Maybe: the chanting sounds dismal and depressing because of the repetition, the alliteration and the words themselves
- Explanation of rhymes like 'ready' and 'steady' which words sound solid and settled – as the slaves are sorted out by the beatings
- Explanations of rhymes like 'praising' and 'raising': uplifting at the end
- The way the rhythm slows with 'up up up' and particularly 'hot slow step' and what this suggests

5 Answer are likely to refer to:

- 'sun coming up' and 'out of the dark'
- how we interpret 'the dumb gods' and their acts
- whether the slaves are rising out of the ship or out of this life
- whether they are arriving in a better place or not
- whether they have been tricked and are in a place that is no better or whether they have actually been saved
- 'hot slow step' and what that suggests
- 'the burning ground' and what it is
- the importance of the full stop at the end and what it suggests
- and how this re-enforces or changes how we read the rest of the poem
- whether this is continuation of their suffering or, finally, relief from it

Extract from a Grade C answer

The ending of the poem is optimistic. After suffering on the ship, the slaves think the music has saved them:

'and the music is saving me'

They are coming 'up, up, up' from below the deck. Earlier, they went 'down, down, down' but the sun has come up, which is a happy thing, and they are 'out of the dark'.

To begin with in the poem, everything was 'silent' and the slaves were stuck below the 'long dark deck'. There, they were beaten ('stick is the whip') and even raped ('knees spread wide').

The song they sang had a rhythm and a beat, to keep them going:

'limbo

limbo like me…'

but at the end they can slow right down: 'hot/slow/step'…

Nothing's Changed

Pages 128–129

1 Answers are likely to include the following:

- Opening line: short, sharp words capture sounds (onomatopoeia) as he walks, e.g. 'hard stones click'
- 'under my heels': maybe sense of being 'down at heel', i.e. poor

- Enjambements (some lines not punctuated at end), moving us on to next line smoothly/quickly, as he moves on
- 'thrust/bearded seeds' – we sense the thrust to the next line
- More onomatopoeia: 'cans, trodden on, crunch'
- Scene of desolation where there used to be life/people living
- Friendly, beautiful weeds at end: maybe like the people who lived there - you do not have to be a rich flower to be beautiful
- 'amiable weeds' all alone, for emphasis, at the end
- All lines broken up, maybe like the black people's world

2 Answers are likely to include:

- 'whites only restaurant': select, exclusive, blacks not allowed
- 'working man's café': contrast – sounds poor, shows who are the workers in the country
- Associated details:
  restaurant – amongst the weeds, like a squatter (should not be there), 'new, up-market, haute cuisine' (for the rich), 'guard at the gatepost' (to keep the unwanted out, 'crushed ice white glass' etc (elegance)
  café – 'bunny chows' (poor man's food), take away or basic tables (not for the well-off), no napkins, and likely to be spit on the floor
- The effects of each detail should be included (reader senses the injustice; responds to each description with feelings of…)
- Explanation of how the effect is achieved (e.g. how we feel about each instance of imagery)

3 Answers are likely to include:

- stanza 1: Afrika returns
- stanza 2: how he feels about District 6
- stanza 3: description of restaurant
- stanza 4: crucial statement of obvious division
- stanza 5: what is inside the restaurant
- stanza 6: contrasted with café
- stanza 7: his emotions and what he would like to do
- It is as if we move with the poet and feel his reactions at each stage
- poem begins with Afrika's trek into District 6 and the description and ends with how he feels about what he has found
- Last line same as title – a circle that continues
- 3 stanzas… 2 lines… 3 stanzas: how the two lines are made central to what is being said

4 Answers are likely to include:

- reasons for the anger
- how it is shown, e.g. repetition in stanza 2, his reaction to the restaurant, etc
- significant details, e.g. what has happened to District 6, the restaurant and the café, his emotions at the end
- close textual references, with their effects
- the ending includes quotes such as:
  – 'boy again'
  – 'small mean'
  – 'Hands burn'
  – 'a bomb'
  – 'shiver down the glass'
  – 'Nothing's changed'

Extract from a Grade C answer

The poet is angry all the way through the poem. We can see why when it starts, because everything is overgrown: 'Small round hard stones click/under my heels'. The words make the sounds of the rough ground, with 'hard' and 'click'. It all sounds very rough. He must want it better, like it used to be. Or maybe like the white people have got it now, in the restaurant we see later. His anger is really shown when he repeats words, and it all builds up in a list that he seems to be saying louder and louder:

'and the skin about my bones,

and the soft labouring of my lungs…'

It comes to a climax when he talks about the 'anger of my eyes'…

Island Man

Pages 130–131

1 Answers are likely to include:

- Man wakes up, in London
- Has been dreaming of his island home in the Caribbean
- We are given the images of his past, what used to be there when he awoke
- He seems unstable/only half awake
- London is very different
- We get the sounds of London
- He drags himself out of bed to face another day in the capital
- The descriptions make it sound as if he is not happy
- He would rather be back in his home

2 Answers should include (with the impression created):

- 'blue surf' – beauty, cleanness
- 'steady breaking and wombing' – sounds, waves and birth
- 'wild seabirds' - freedom
- 'fishermen' – in touch with natural world
- 'sun surfacing defiantly' – alliteration: smoothness
- 'small emerald island' – sounds like a jewel
- 'grey metallic soar' – sounds industrialised and play on words (soar/sore)
- 'surge of wheels' – sounds
- 'dull North Circular roar' – sounds again plus lack of real life (dull)

3
- *the steady breaking and wombing* – sense of calm, waves coming in, effect of 'wombing' (birth)
- *he always comes back   groggily groggily* – gap shows how his mind stops for a moment; repeated 'groggily' emphasises his confusion/state of mind
- *Comes back to sands*
- *of a grey metallic roar* – contrast in two lines (second unexpected); colour and 'metallic' so unlike what an island offers
- *island man heaves himself*
- *Another London day* – effect of 'heaves': real effort; space leaves him more time to think; simple bluntness of what he faces

4 Opening:

- Beautiful impression of Caribbean
- Presents all that he has lost
- Details to be examined

Ending:

- 'muffling muffling' as if he is trying to cut out reality
- 'crumpled' unpleasant – closest he gets now to waves
- The huge effort to just get out of bed
- Dismal impression of final line

5 Answers are likely to include:

- Lines create impression of waves
- Sense of impressions coming and going, with the lines
- Effect created by space before 'groggily groggily'
- Final line isolated, for effect
- Only punctuation is capital letters – which shows starting points ('Morning', 'Comes back' and 'Another')

- And also shows the heaviness of important features: 'North Circular' and 'London'
- Lack of other punctuation allows fluidity – which might once have been the on-going motion of the waves, but is now the ceaseless sounds of the city or the endless days in London

Blessing

Pages 132–133

1 Answers are likely to include:

- 'The skin cracks like a pod' – simile - suggests dryness, people are suffering like the crops
- 'There never is enough water' – blunt statement of fact
- 'Imagine the drip of it' – onomatopoeia; and the sense that it can only be imagined – it is the stuff of dreams
- 'the small splash, echo' – onomatopoeia; and 'echo', as if the imagination keeps returning to the imagined sound
- 'the voice of a kindly god' – as if water comes from god and just a small drop would seem like an enormous gift

2 Possible ideas of how religion is brought into the poem:

- Suggested initially by 'voice of a kindly god'
- A 'roar of tongues' almost like a religious outpouring
- People rushing out for water are 'a congregation'
- The idea of a 'blessing'

3 Words and their effect:

- 'voice of a kindly god'
- 'sudden rush of fortune' – as if someone has struck gold
- 'silver' – sense of value
- 'liquid sun' – giving life
- How everyone rushes to collect the valuable commodity (details of the crowds or all that they use to collect the water, so none is wasted)
- The idea of 'blessing'

4 Answers are likely to refer to:

- sentence rushes on because the people are so excited and there is so much happening
- no stop until the end
- 'man woman child' tumble together, without even a comma

11

- listing shows enthusiasm, mood
- anything will do to collect water
- 'frantic hands'
- 'screaming'
- sense of richness for the moment
- 'polished to perfection'
- 'flashing light'
- children identified as having real fun and 'blessing sings over their small bones'

Extract from a Grade C answer

There is one long sentence to end the poem because it all happens so suddenly, so there is no stopping for the people and the sentence just runs on. We know the people are happy because they are a 'congregation', like you would find in church, and the children are 'screaming in the liquid sun' – probably screaming with joy. We also know that they are rushing around because of the list thee poet uses, explaining what the people use to collect the water, and the way we are told about how they 'butt in' and have 'frantic hands'. They must be really desperate for the relief the water will give them...

5 The title of the poem is appropriate:

- Because they feel blessed – maybe their lives have been saved
- Because of the religious significance
- Because they are likely to see it as God's doing

Two Scavengers in a Truck, Two Beautiful People in a Mercedes

Pages 134–135

1 Answers are likely to include:

- Wearing 'red plastic blazers'
- Hanging on to the garbage truck
- Up since 4 am
- Dirty but on their way home
- How the older man is described – close detail
- How the younger man is described – close detail
- They are looking down into the Mercedes

2 Answers are likely to include:

- Man very trendy – 'hip'
- Wears a suit
- Long haired, with sunglasses, appearing 'cool'

- An architect, who does not have to begin work early
- Woman young, blond, with hair that has been made to seem 'casually' got ready
- Short skirt and coloured stockings, seeming to have made herself attractive
- Apparently works with him (secretary?)
- Both seem as if out of a TV advertisement ('odourless', as if removed from reality)

3 They are contrasted by:

- Transport
- Clothing
- General appearance
- Life styles
- Younger men have things in common, but...
- Older man 'gargoyle Quasimodo' contrasts with girl, as partner of younger man
- They are a 'distance' apart
- Only together for an instant

4 Answers are likely to include:

- To show the shifting nature of society
- To show how society is broken into bits that only just manage to hang together
- To represent waves 'in the high seas of this democracy'
- To show how the vehicles are edging forwards at the lights
- And it affects how we read the poem: we break it into the units that are lines, so that, for example:
- 'and looking down into

  an elegant Mercedes'
- makes us pause, as perhaps, the garbage men pause; and our eyes drop, like theirs, as we move to the next line.

5 Answers are likely to suggest:

- The American Dream is still possible – everyone has a chance

or

- They only meet for an instant: it is 'as if anything at all were possible', but it is not
- Answers likely to hinge on the interpretation of the 'small gulf' (which is an oxymoron - a contradiction in terms)
- There might be comment on the layout and how that suggests a coming together or drifting apart – especially looking at the final lines

Language is likely to range across:

- 'odourless TV ad'
- 'everything is always possible'/'anything at all were possible'

- 'an instant'
- 'small gulf'
- 'in the high seas of this democracy'

Night of the Scorpion

Pages 136–137

1 Answers are likely to include:

- First person narrative, which make sit all seem real
- Chronological – in the order that it happens
- Conversational from the start, as if talking to a friend
- Quoting and describing just how it happened
- Moving to significant final three lines – which is the only time the mother speaks

2 Answers are likely to include:

- We know it is in the Third World and people are poor – 'a sack of rice'
- Rainy season
- No electric lights – 'dark room' and 'candles/lanterns'
- Mud-baked walls', so probably huts
- Sit on floor
- Insects and scorpion so somewhere hot

3 Answers are likely to include:

- Starts with statement of what happens
- Main section ends with an equally simple statement
- Ends with mother's words, as she recovers
- Takes us through chronologically, so we see the incidents in the order they happened
- Attempts to save her becoming more extreme, through neighbours' prayers to rites of holy man, to husband trying things in which he does not believe, then trying to burn the poison away

4 Answer is likely to refer to:

Peasants:
- 'like swarms of flies'
- buzzed the name of God…'
- 'with candles and with lanterns…'
- 'They clicked their tongues'
- what they said
- what they believed
- sat around mother
- more of them

Father:
- 'sceptic, rationalist'
- 'trying every…'
- the paraffin
- Holy man:
- his rites
- and incantation

All the people care enough about the mother to try to help her. First there are the neighbours. We find out they are peasants but they might have been a bit annoying because they came 'like swarms of flies'. There is also a metaphor, when they 'buzzed the name of God a hundred times'. Ezekiel tries to make it sound as if they are muttering together but he is still thinking of them as flies. They are like the sound of flies in the air. Of course, all they want to do is deal with the scorpion. They are very religious, because they think of the scorpion as 'the Evil One. It is being presented as the devil…

Vultures

Pages 138–139

1 Section 1

- Miserable dawn
- Two vultures on a dead tree
- Description of male
- His head 'inclined' to hers
- Yesterday they ate the dead animal
- They still kept what was left in sight afterwards

Section 2

- Contemplates the strangeness of love
- In many ways it is very 'particular'
- But will put up with dreadful things, make the most of them and even pretend they do not exist

Section 3

- This is linked to the Commandant at Belson
- Has fumes of human roast in his nostrils
- Stops on way home to buy chocolate for his 'his tender offspring'
- They wait at home for the man who is simply their 'Daddy'

Section 4

- Contemplates the contradictions
- Be pleased that even the worst have had goodness within them
- Or despair because even love harbours evil

2 Answer is likely to refer to:

- atmosphere at the start and how it is created e.g. 'greyness', 'drizzle', 'despondent dawn' etc
- the tree and the description of the male vulture
- what the vultures eat
- vocabulary like 'charnel house'
- how love is presented
- the contrasts in the Commandant's life
- the ideas in the final section of the poem
- how the long sentences run on like all the horror in this life seems to run on
- possibly mentioning enjambments, where lines run on to the next to create a particular effect e.g. 'cold/telescopic eyes' so the 'cold' and the 'telescopic eyes' are both given prominence as the phrase slows down

Extract from a Grade C answer

From the start, the poem is depressing. The words create the mood: 'greyness', 'drizzle' and 'despondent'. Even the alliteration 'drizzle of one despondent dawn' uses dreary 'd' sounds. This is not a happy opening to the day. The vultures are on a 'dead tree', which further develops the miserable idea, and the branch they are sitting on is described with an unpleasant, painful metaphor: 'broken bone'. If that was all not bad enough, the atmosphere is made worse by the poet telling us about what they have been doing; 'Yesterday they picked the eyes of a swollen corpse…' He tries to upset us by saying they also 'ate the things in its bowel' which is a disgusting idea…

3 Answers are likely to include opinions based in detail upon:

- what the male vulture looks like
- what they have done and are doing
- their relationship

4 Answers are likely to include:

- A evil creation: 'fumes of human roast…'
- Even mentioning his 'hairy nostrils'
- Caring about his child/children when he is so awful to others
- Contrast: chocolate/human roast
- 'Daddy' but a monster

5 Answers are likely to include:

- analysis of the relationship between the vultures
- the love and hate that are part of the Commandant

- how love might well ignore what it finds distasteful
- it is good that even evil creatures can love
- it is tragic that even in love, there still exists evil

What Were They Like?

Pages 140–141

1 Answers are likely to include:

- 2 sections: questions and answers
- Questions present images of Viet Nam as it was
- Answers explain what has happened to it
- Poem can be read from line 1 through to the end
- Or we can read a question, then its answer, and so on: either way makes sense
- Organisation gives clear sense of how it has been transformed: then and now
- It also gives impression that people have forgotten what it was like – hence the questions

2 Answer is likely to include:

- shows respect of Vietnamese people to others
- it is as if a child is speaking to someone who should be their teacher
- it is like a soldier talking – one who has seen the reality

3 Answer is likely to refer to:

- simple and maybe artistic ('lanterns of stone')
- religious ('ceremonies')
- closeness with nature ('to reverence the opening of buds')
- peaceful and happy ('quiet laughter')
- full of beautiful artefacts ('bone and ivory…')
- lives full of poetry, perhaps ('epic poem')
- as if all their life was harmonious ('Did they distinguish…')
- answers likely to state or imply the feelings of the people and the general nature of their society

Extract from a Grade C answer

It seems as if life was good before the war. The people seem to have had a pleasant time, even if their life was very simple. They did not have electric lights, but 'lanterns of stone'. These sound old but solid and dependable. They were also worshipping nature:

'Did they hold ceremonies

to reverence the opening of buds.'

'Buds' make it sound like there were lots of new things growing all the time and 'reverence' lets us know that the people were respectful of what nature gave them…

4   Answer should refer to the fact that the answers to the questions present an alternative viewpoint and might well deal with:

- 'stone': now light hearts and lanterns forgotten
- 'buds' now no more and representing children too
- mouths now burned so don't laugh (napalm?)
- no ornaments because no joy; and bones all burned
- poetry was of an oral tradition, told by fathers to sons – but all their life was destroyed (answers should include details) so no one now knows
- image of 'moths in moonlight' – frail and soon gone; and all is silent now

Extract from a Grade C answer

Each answer in the second half of the poem presents both peace and war. Usually there is some detail of each, though in number 4 we just get 'Laughter is bitter to the burned mouth'. Here the laughter of peace is set against the pain and horror of war. The alliteration of 'bitter' and 'burned' sounds sharp and angry.

The first answer talks about light hearts turning to stone. Through the metaphor the poet shows the weight that fell on the people. It is even as if their memories have been wiped away. Their 'pleasant ways' seem a thing of the past – and this suggests both the paths in the land but also the ways they lived their happy lives. The death of the children mentioned in answer number 2 links the children to nature. They were buds that failed to re-appear after the war.

'Perhaps they gathered once to delight in blossom'

reminds the reader of what life must have been like once, but it seems a long time ago and it is as if it might never have happened…

5   Answers should mention the final five lines and might suggest:

- Probably a sense of depression and devastation:
  'Who can say? It is silent now'

- However, there is still something of their culture, somewhere:
  'There is an echo yet…'
- and the beauty of their existence:
  'speech which was like a song'
- What has been lost was fragile and beautiful:
  'their singing resembled
  the flight of moths in moonlight'
- And the reader is left to lament their passing
- And the fact that so little about them is known ('Who can say?')

from Search For My Tongue

Pages 142–143

1   Answer is likely to include:

- Identity is important
- Problems arise when you move to another country, which speaks a different language
- Even when you think you have lost it, your 'mother tongue' stays with you
- The language in this poem represents the identity of Bhatt
- The language represents her culture

2   Answer is likely to refer to:

- tongue as identity, link with past and culture
- the two tongues
- how the mother tongue struggles in a foreign land
- the rotting
- 'I thought I spit it out'
- the Gujerati
- how the mother tongue is sandwiched between the English
- the re-growth and its strength
- the blossoming
- how language is used to put across the poet's message

Extract from a Grade C answer

Sujata Bhatt uses the idea of her tongue to represent where she came from. It is her original culture. At first she thinks she has lost it and she challenges the reader by asking how we would cope:

'I ask you, what would you do..?'

Having involved us in her problem, she explains how the mother tongue was important to her because even when she has lost it, she still doesn't seem a part of her new environment, saying she 'could not really know the other, the foreign tongue'. The word 'foreign' stresses how difficult this is for her. It is as if she struggles to say anything at all, as if she has actually 'lost her tongue'…

3 Answer is likely to suggest:

- it shows us how she spoke in her own country
- it brings to life her culture and way of speaking
- it forces its way into the poem, just as it does into her dreams
- as we struggle to read it, we understand her problems in our country
- it is stuck between English sections, just as she feels surrounded in England

4 Answers might include points such as:

- Direct opening, talking to reader
- As if part of conversation
- Rhetorical question
- Second person approach
- Conversational throughout
- We are expected to read the Gujerati

5 Answer is likely to refer to:

- repeated 'grows'
- impression created by vocabulary like 'longer', 'moist', 'strong veins'
- metaphor of victory: 'ties other tongue in knots'
- sense of opening, new beginning
- 'bud' equals new life
- 'opens' repeated for emphasis
- it is stronger: 'pushes other tongue aside'
- contrast to 'forgotten' – 'blossoms'
- idea of flowering, something beautiful growing, etc
- sense of summer

Extract from a Grade C answer

The tongue grows back. To emphasise that, the word 'grows' is repeated and seems to build up to a climax: 'it ties the other tongue in knots'. The mother tongue is in control now. To show that it is growing, there is then the phrase 'the bud opens'. This sounds like a new beginning, and even thought he tongue is still just a bud it is strong enough to push aside the foreign tongue. By the end, everything has gone well and the bud is starting to 'blossom'…

from Unrelated Incidents

Pages 144–145

1 Answers are likely to include:

- He does not like them
- They think they are superior and speak correctly
- Their correct speech suggests to people that what they say is true
- He dislikes the idea that only those who speak correctly actually understand what is true

2 Answers are likely to include:

- They think they are inferior
- They see those with regional accents as 'scruffs'
- They think do not know what is true
- And ordinary people cannot be believed
- They think only those who write and speak correctly are to be trusted
- The speaker does not accept people's prejudices

3 Answers are likely to suggest:

- Truth is usually expected to come from people with the 'right way' of talking
- 'right tokn' and 'spellin' should not be a guide to what is true
- We each have a right to 'trooth'
- Any of us can claim we have the truth and others don't – we can claim that our truth and way of speaking is actually correct

4 Answers are likely to include:

- the language indicates a different culture from what is accepted as 'normal'
- the speaker is not part of formal English society
- he seems to be angry and frustrated by the way people judge him
- unusual spellings and analysis
- unconventional features (things that are not normally accepted) in the way it is written e.g. punctuation and even line length

5 Answers are likely to refer to:

- Like an autocue, with its link to a BBC announcer and the fact that this way of speaking is an alternative
- Opening like a news broadcast
- Change into Scottish accent
- Lack of punctuation to begin
- 'this is the six a…': contrast at end with 'thi'

- 'news' and 'nyooz'
- 'talk wia BBC accent' and 'yi canny talk right'
- Repetition, start and end
- Effect of 'belt up'

Since the poem is about a Scotsman complaining about the BBC accents that are heard on the news, it is fitting that it is set out like an autocue. It starts off with a newsreader saying:

'this is thi

six a clock

news...'

and there are just three words on each line, as there might be on the autocue: there are two or three words per line throughout the poem to maintain this impression.

The poem starts and ends with 'this is the six a clock nyooz', although it is spelt differently in each case, as if spelling (and, Leonard thinks, accent too) is not important. However, the final two words are 'belt up'. This suggests that the poet is sick of hearing 'proper English'. The message has been delivered and there is nothing more to say...

6 Answers are likely to refer to:

- Showing that what is conventional is not actually required
- Showing that it is still fine to be different – you can still be understood
- Demonstrating a lack of respect for conventions
- Likely to illustrate all ideas with close detail from poem
- Likely to demonstrate how the accent comes through the spelling
- Likely to show how the lines in which it is written help the reader towards
- understanding, so punctuation is not always needed in any case

The spelling and the punctuation are trying to make the reader understand that the poet is different. It gives us an idea of how he is feeling and how he speaks. In fact, we can reproduce his words when we read how they are written:

'yi widny wahnt mi ti talk'.

We are automatically made to speak Glaswegian. This goes on right through the poem and it is done on purpose because the poet can sound more like he is speaking standard English when he wants, like at the start when he says 'this is thi six a clock news'. The spelling lets us know that he is different, but the words themselves sound English ...

Half-Caste

Pages 146–147

1 Answers are likely to suggest:

- Everyone is the same, regardless of their colour
- People who us the term 'half-caste' are stupid/racist
- The term implies that someone of mixed race is only half a person, which is clearly not the case
- There are many mixes of colour in things in the world, but they are not considered 'half-caste'
- Those who see mixed race people as 'half-caste' are really the limited ones – using only half their intelligence

2 Answers are likely to include:

- To capture the way John Agard talks
- To challenge the reader
- To make it sound like an argument or conversation
- Mention of irony/sarcasm, to attack the ways people see 'half-caste' individuals

3 Answers are likely to include:

- Makes poet sound persistent ('explain', 'explain'...)
- Repeats the question because people do not seem to have an answer ('what yu mean...')
- 'mix' is repeated to stress how much mixing there is in the world, apart from mixed race people
- 'half' repeated because it is the central idea
- 'and when...' repeated to show how this involves all of his life, not just a part
- 'the whole' repeated at the end because a whole is the ideal

4 Answers are likely to include:

- He is called 'half-caste' so he reveals how other things that are mixed do not suffer the same fate
- He chooses a natural thing (England weather)
- And things of beauty (Picasso's paintings, Tchaikovsky's symphony)

- He ridicules the idea that he only perceives through 'half of mih ear' etc
- He makes fun of the fact that it might be supposed he only lives half a life
- And that he has still only told half of his story at the end

5 Answers are likely to include:

- Lines help us read the poem – they make sense of the words for us
- Capitals open sections of the poem
- Lack of punctuation generally is an indication that the speaker is not seen as the same as most people
- Shows that you can be a little different but still be of value
- Where the speaker pauses there is a /, to give us that indication
- Lack of punctuation generally shows that this problem has no natural stop – it just goes on and on

6 Answers are likely to include:

- It is as if the listener/reader is being dismissed – and should come back with a more open mind
- It is not the speaker who is 'half', but the listener
- The lack of wholeness is stressed by the repetition of 'de whole of yu...'
- And the mind is the third 'half' in the list – the most important item, because only half the brain seems to have been working
- Final lines suggest poet is still willing to educate the listener, once the listener opens his mind
- Final joke – there are two halves to his story

Love After Love

Pages 148–149

1 Answers are likely to include:

- Presumably a relationship has failed ('whom you ignored for another')
- So now he has to learn how to love again
- Only this time it is how to love himself and what he is
- This true self has been a lover in the background, throughout life
- This love and understanding of self is what has been forgotten through the relationship and is the 'love after love'

2 Answers are likely to include:

- Enthusiastically
- Directly: 'you'
- Like someone encouraging the reader to be positive
- As someone offering advice, instruction: 'Sit. Feast on your life.'
- As someone offering a brighter future

3 Answers are likely to include:

- They are very direct – commanding
- They make all the advice seem very simple
- 'Give wine. Give bread': the echo of Christianity, perhaps
- 'Sit. Feast on your life': like the owner of a restaurant, welcoming diners.

4 Answers are likely to refer to:

- A house: 'at your own door, in your own mirror'
- Friendly place: 'each will smile...'
- Ideas of what has happened here: 'love letters from the bookshelf'
- There has been a history: 'The photographs, the desperate notes'
- A place that is rich in life: 'Feast on your life'

5 Answers are likely to refer to:

- choice of vocabulary: 'elation', 'greet', 'smile', 'welcome'
- long sentence to open – enthusiasm
- friendly welcome and offer: simple and kind: 'Eat.'
- importance of 'love again'
- religious vocabulary; wine and bread
- returning to original love: 'Give you're your heart'
- sense of change at the end – removing what is past and changing to optimism
- final line: sense of relish, as 'Eat' has changed to 'Feast'

Extract from a Grade C answer

The poem starts happily, since the first verse ends with 'And each will smile at the other's welcome'. There is 'elation' too. This word suggests more than just quiet pleasure. It suggests great joy.

Right at the end, we have: 'Sit. Feast on your life.' This is also very positive. We are not told to just eat, but to feast. This word gives an impression of lots of food, as if for a celebration, like a birthday. We picture heaps of good food.

Right through the poem the poet is telling the reader what to do to make sure life is good. We get instructions like 'Eat', 'Give wine. Give bread'. Because some of this reminds us of the Bible, it all seems like a fine religious experience...

This room

Pages 150–151

1 Answers are likely to include:

- A room representing delight and life
- Sense of things expanding, tearing apart
- Uplift
- Celebration
- Excitement
- Joy

2 Answers are likely to include:

- Verbs: 'breaking', 'cracking through'
- Enjambements, as the lines run on to emphasise excitement
- Idea of moving onward, upward to a better place: 'in search of space, light...'
- Bed shifting form nightmares, presumably into dreamland
- 'dark corners' left behind
- Chairs are 'rising up'
- This is an exciting escape; 'crash through clouds'

3 Answers are likely to include:

- 'daily furniture of our lives stirs'
- 'pots and pans bang together'
- 'clang past'
- 'the crowd of garlic, onions, spices'
- 'a' sounds
- How the enjambements give emphasis to the words that begin the next line

4 Answers are likely to refer to:

- details within the house
- what happens to the items in the house
- nightmares and dark corners gone
- positive verbs – often of sound and movement
- cluster of impressions, movement, bustle
- onomatopoeia
- enjambments
- 'excitement' at end – and growing from what has come earlier e.g. 'This is the time and place to be alive'
- 'clapping' – applause for what has happened

The poem makes it seem the room is bursting apart. Everything is flying around. It is all very exciting:

'This is the time and place
to be alive'

The fact that 'No one is looking for the door' because this is all so wonderful. The poet is so thrilled that he hardly knows where he is:

'I'm wondering where
I've left my feet'

but he is certainly happy:

'my hands are outside, clapping.'

The enjambements try to emphasise this excitement. We are told:

'This room is breaking out
of itself'

and even the line is broken...

5 Answers are likely to include:

- Happy ending
- As if everything is being pulled into exciting pieces (line separated from previous verse)
- Emphasis on final word – a verb: 'clapping'
- Which is onomatopoeia and suggests applause because something has gone well
- Sense of escape to conclude

Not My Business

Pages 152–153

1 Answers are likely to include:

- Akanni
- Danladi
- Chinwe
- The speaker in the poem

2 Answers are likely to include:

- Regular stanzas with familiar pattern
- To mirror familiar situations arising in the country
- Each situation with individuals followed by three line chorus from speaker, repeating how he is not getting involved
- Significant final stanza, as his turn comes
- Use of jeep at start and finish
- Change in situation with regard to yam at end
- His silence mirrored by jeep at end

3 Answers are likely to include:

- Knows exactly what happens to Akanni, Danladi and Chinwe
- Ignores them, to concentrate on his yam, on himself
- Repeated chorus to stress his attitude
- At end, it all changes
- His 'hungry hand' – which emphasises how he cares about his own welfare and needs –
- Is 'frozen', showing how things are about to change and showing his fear
- Presumably he, like his lawn, is 'bewildered'
- He is intimidated by the waiting jeep

4 Answers should include:

- To show how he refuses to become involved
- To show how much he is ignoring
- To remind us of his lack of care for others or fear for himself

5 Answers are likely to include:

'Beat him soft…'
- Simile: response to the idea he is beaten soft, so all bones broken, or until he is senseless/has no strength left
- 'stuffed' like something of no importance
- Jeep sounds like a hungry animal (metaphor of belly)

'Booted…'
- Violence of image
- And no way of avoiding it (metaphor – whole house wakened)

'No query…'
- Straightforward list; no way it can be changed
- Negativity: 'no'
- No rights for the unfortunate victims

'The jeep was waiting…'
- Sense of being 'bewildered' (metaphor)
- 'waiting, waiting' – patient and there will be no escape
- Silence threatening

Presents from my Aunts in Pakistan

Pages 154–155

1 Answers are likely to say things like:

- She is torn between two cultures, of 'no fixed nationality'
- She does not feel at ease with either
- The clothes illustrate the different cultures
- Has only distant memories of Pakistan

- But the items around her keep that culture alive, even if she does not feel she fits with it
- Likes English clothes, but not free to express herself fully

2 Answers are likely to include:

- The items around her represent that culture
- Clothes seem beautiful to her
- Bangles hurt her, literally and, perhaps, metaphorically
- 'alien' in the clothes
- 'couldn't rise up out of its fire'
- Camel-skin lamp: has been transformed but still beautiful
- Mother's jewellery stolen – loss of culture?
- School friend not impressed by clothes
- She admired them
- Remembers conflict in Pakistan, like conflict in herself
- Aunts – screened in their culture
- Beggars at the bottom of the caste system – and she herself feels excluded from the best, staring through fretwork

3 Some possible points:

- Doesn't feel comfortable in Pakistani clothes
- 'alien', 'couldn't rise up out of its fire'
- Longs for 'denim and corduroy'
- 'half-English'
- Maybe like the lamp, wants to be transformed

4 Answer are likely to refer to:

- the salwar kameez; colours, simile, etc
- the slippers
- the bangles
- the apple green sari
- satin-silken tops
- the lamp
- the jewellery
- the mirror-work
- memories of Pakistan
- the aunts
- the beggars
- and to comment on how the colour, imagery etc bring to life the culture for the reader

Extract from a Grade C answer

The poet gives us a clear picture of what the girl's life is like. We know about her Pakistani clothes, for example. The salwar kameez is peacock blue, which is bright and cheerful, and another is 'glistening like an orange split open'. In this case, we have lovely colour again, but also it seems linked to fruit and the beauty of nature. Then:

'My aunts chose an apple-green sari

    silver bordered...'

Once more we have fruit, and now richness too. The texture is also made clear ('satin-silken'). The Pakistani culture seems vibrant.

We know about other things too. They have a camel-skin lamp in the house, which sounds unpleasant to begin with, but actually has 'colours/like stained glass'...

5 Answers are likely to suggest:

- She feels like an outsider
- as shown by 'staring through fretwork'
- Mention of beggars, sweeper girls, implies, that she, like them, feels a sense of exclusion
- 'of no fixed nationality' presents her situation
- 'Shalimar Gardens' at the end: significant place in Pakistan but she can only see it from a distance
- Presents her problems

Hurricane Hits England

Pages 156–157

1 Answers are likely to include:

- She has moved from the Caribbean to England
- She has not felt settled in England
- But then a hurricane arrives
- At first she is confused about what is happening
- But it reminds her of home
- And she then realises that being in England is like being at home
- She feels freed from her worries and isolation
- She warms to life again
- And that all places are similar, all just parts of the earth

2 Answers are likely to refer to:

- first through the poet's presentation of the storm ('howling ship', etc) and her wakefulness: presumably she is worried/afraid
- then through her questioning of the gods
- her balancing of the 'illumination' and the 'darkness'
- the rhetorical questioning about what is happening
- 'unchained' – the transformation for her
- her links with the weather and what it means
- the 'frozen lake' in her has gone
- she recognises that you can live and warm anywhere: 'the earth is the earth'

At the beginning of the poem, Nichols seems unhappy in England. When the hurricane arrives, she lies awake. It sounds as though she might be frightened. There is the metaphor of the 'howling ship', which could come from a nightmare. Also, the storm seems angry ('gathering rage') and seems like a ghost that has come to get her – 'some dark ancestral spectre'. She has moved countries, and we think that the ghosts have come to punish her. However, they are not just 'fearful', they are also 'reassuring'. The poet shows that she has two reactions to what is happening. Because she knows that this is what she was used to in the Caribbean, she can communicate with the storm, calling on the gods she knew...

3 Answers are likely to include:

- The storms can come in either place
- The devastation will be the same in England as in the Caribbean
- Caribbean imagery (of ships etc) applied to English setting
- The trees falling remind her of whales
- It is as if the gods are in both places
- 'the earth is the earth is the earth'

4 Answers are likely to include:

- Relieved and relaxed
- Grateful to the storm and what it means
- Describes it as 'sweet mystery'
- Her 'frozen' nature has now gone
- Metaphorically her foundations have been shaken and she is alive again
- There is a new philosophy for her in the final line – she now knows that everywhere is part of one earth

5 Answers are likely to refer to:

- 'ancestral spectre'
- 'Huracan, Oya, Shango, Hattie'
- 'old tongues /Reaping havoc /In new places'
- 'whales'
- winds and storms

and how the concepts are presented, such as:
- 'howling ship of the wind' (onomatopoeia and metaphor)
- the 'darkness' of the ancestral spectre – suggesting evil, perhaps, and something to inspire fear
- 'My sweeping, back-home cousin' – sounding welcomed and as part of the family

- enjambement in 'old tongues…' so that each part of the sentence is stressed, giving an almost breathless sensation

We know that her life used to be very different to the one she now lives. The gods she worshipped are identified: Hurracan, Oya, Shango and Hattie. These names show how different it all was to English culture. We know she came from a country where there were hurricanes that were accepted as a part of life – maybe even as a part of the family ('my sweeping, back-home cousin'). This makes the storms seem important and you might be 'fearful' but you should not be terrified because the storm can be 'reassuring'. When trees are uprooted, it makes Nichols think of whales, and that suggests that she lived close to the sea. She was obviously 'at one' with nature in her old life, because when the storm arrives she is happy with it: 'I am riding the mystery of your storm'…

Comparing poems answers

Pages 158–159

Cluster 1

1 An effective introduction should:

   • Deal with the title – 'how' and 'relationships' and might:
   • Make at least one point about each poem
   • Involve a comparison of some kind

2 Comparisons can be found in the ideas, in the language or in the structure.

3 The conclusion might:

   • Clearly re-state the main points of comparison
   • And/or summarise how relationships are presented

4 The precise nature of the content will depend upon which poem you have chosen as a comparison.

   The *Night of the Scorpion* section is likely to deal with:

   • how the poet presents the mother i.e. how they relate to each other

   • the neighbours and their involvement
   • the father
   • the holy man
   • the mother's final words

Pages 160–161

Cluster 2

1 Answer is likely to include:

   • he is in a country in which people are being persecuted unfairly
   • he keeps himself to himself and does not get involved
   • he is concerned with his own life/own appetite
   • finally, though, the jeep comes for him

2 Answer should deal with the language and, ideally, link with the speaker's situation, e.g. 'my savouring mouth': he is happy just eating and focuses on his appetite rather than his neighbours' problems; his mouth is watering as they suffer. What is happening to them is a part of his situation, so comments might be based around the suffering of Akanni, Danladi and Chinwe.

3 Try to make at least two points and remember to back them up with details from the poem.

4 You would earn one mark for each valid comment which deals with the language and, ideally, links with the speaker's situation.

5 Content will depend upon which poem you have chosen as a comparison.

   The *Not My Business* section is likely to deal with:

   • the neighbours and what happens to them
   • the speaker's reaction to their problems
   • the state of the country
   • how his situation is transformed at the end
   Importantly, there should also be a close focus on **how** language is used in the poems.

Writing answers

No two people will write the same answer to questions of the sort contained within this Exam Practice Workbook – or indeed in your GCSE exam. There is no such thing as a right or wrong answer, but in order to achieve certain grades at GCSE you will be expected to demonstrate certain skills in your writing.

The following grid gives you some general guidelines. If you visit www.collinseducation.com/revision, you will find grids and guidance that relate more specifically to individual questions.

Grade	Possible content
F/G	• content which has some link with the topic • unlikely to be suitable for purpose and audience • fails to interest • some accurate spelling of simple words but likely to be little accurate punctuation • unlikely to use any higher quality language features
E	• content attempts to introduce the topic effectively • attempts suitability for the purpose and audience • attempts to interest • some accurate spelling and punctuation • some attempt at higher quality language features
D	• content addresses the topic • some suitability for the purpose and audience • some interest for the reader • generally accurate spelling and punctuation • a few higher quality language features
C	• content is appropriate • acceptable for the intended purpose and audience • interests the reader • mostly accurate spelling and punctuation • uses appropriate high quality language features
B	• content is both appropriate and well organised • appropriate for the intended purpose and audience • likely to hold the reader's interest • mostly accurate spelling of a suitable vocabulary • a range of generally accurate punctuation • effective use of linguistic devices
A/A*	• content is appropriate, well organised and convincing • totally suitable for the intended purpose and audience • likely to grab and hold the reader's interest • accurate spelling of an advanced but appropriate vocabulary • a range of accurate punctuation • original and effective use of linguistic devices